TRANSFORMING
THE ORDINARY

Text copyright © John Henstridge 2004
The author asserts the moral right
to be identified as the author of this work

Published by
The Bible Reading Fellowship
First Floor, Elsfield Hall
15–17 Elsfield Way, Oxford OX2 8FG

ISBN 1 84101 316 1
First published 2004
10 9 8 7 6 5 4 3 2 1 0

Acknowledgments
Unless otherwise stated, scripture quotations are taken from The New Revised
Standard Version of the Bible, Anglicized Edition, copyright © 1989, 1995 by the
Division of Christian Education of the National Council of the Churches of Christ
in the USA, and are used by permission. All rights reserved.

Material from *The Alternative Service Book 1980* is copyright © The Central Board of
Finance of the Church of England.

A catalogue record for this book is available from the British Library

Printed and bound in Great Britain by
Bookmarque, Croydon

TRANSFORMING
THE ORDINARY

BIBLE MEDITATIONS FOR THE EVERYDAY

JOHN HENSTRIDGE

ACKNOWLEDGMENTS AND DEDICATION

All prayer is a gift from God, and we who receive this gift are abundantly blessed. This collection of meditations is no exception. It all began when I was hanging out some washing (we run a modest B & B) and wondering what on earth it was all about. Then, as I hung up a towel, a picture came into my mind of Jesus—how he took a towel, put it around himself, and washed the feet of his disciples. The action then became invested with the presence of Jesus. How helpful it would be for us as Christians to have a reflective picture from the Bible in all our activities! So began God's gift for this book of meditations.

God has also gifted this book through the help and support of others. Some have supported me with their prayers, especially Mary Fardell, Dom Timothy, OSB, and Jennifer Rees Larcombe. Naomi Starkey, BRF Editor, has been supportive as always and, with her usual perception, showed how to put the meditations into a usable form. Archbishop Rowan Williams has been encouraging, and generous in writing the Foreword, so full of spiritual insight. My daughter-in-law, Catherine, has given much time to use her considerable expertise and Christian insight, not only in proofreading and the correction of my countless errors in grammar and punctuation, but also in many constructive suggestions for the use of language and the content.

Finally, my family has, as always, been a great support, especially my wife, Prue, who has been patient and understanding.

To all of these people this book is dedicated. Any faults are entirely my own; all that is good comes from God to whom be glory and praise. May he bless all who use these meditations with his love and joy and grace.

CONTENTS

FOREWORD

Perhaps the biggest breakthrough in our understanding of prayer is when we stop thinking of it as if it were something we were doing so as to attract the attention of someone far off. It's all too easy to be misled by the language we sometimes use, not to mention the strange ideas about God that most of us have lurking somewhere in our minds. God's in his heaven (so he's not here); God is holy and pure (so he won't like the look of *me*); God has to be approached with great care and caution (and I haven't got the time). The best I can do is to wave nervously from a distance from time to time, slightly hoping I don't actually get noticed.

The trouble is that this completely ignores the very heart of the New Testament, the revolution in thinking about prayer that comes through both the teaching and the work of Jesus. His teaching, specially in the Sermon on the Mount, makes it clear that God is eagerly waiting for our company, and that he is already more intimately involved with us than we can imagine. But the effects of Jesus' death and resurrection and the sending of the Holy Spirit make things still clearer. What happens when we pray is part of what happens in the whole of our lives as believers—Jesus comes to life in us and acts though our actions and words. And so, when we say 'Our Father', it's not just because Jesus had this nice idea that it would be helpful to call God Father; it's because we really do share Jesus' own relationship to the God from whom he comes.

Prayer is quite inseparable from simply living in and with Jesus. In that sense, it's always going on and we can 'tune in' to it at any point, in any place. There's no great journey to go on, no elaborate conditions to be met, no problems in getting God to listen. But that also means that the best way to grow in prayer is to give ourselves time to be able to 'tune in', to become just a bit more aware of the mystery of Jesus' life in us.

What John Henstridge's reflections do is to help us with just this tuning in—using our imaginations to bring the presence of Jesus to light in the present moment, and using quiet and stillness to let that presence flower in our minds and hearts. These pages are wonderfully accessible for everyone, and I know that they will lead many towards a fuller recognition of the God who has already crossed the gap between heaven and earth and who is always waiting for us in the depth of our hearts, in the depths of the present moment.

Rowan Williams, Archbishop of Canterbury

INTRODUCTION

Look towards him and be bright with joy. (Psalm 34:5, ASB)

As you look back on almost any experience, you may well ask, 'Where was God in all that?' or, 'Was Jesus there?' We know quite well from the Gospels that Jesus is always with us, wherever we are, whatever we are doing, whatever we are thinking or feeling. That is his promise. But do we remember? Are we aware of his presence?

Sometimes we remember, and may say a prayer or a word of thanks. All too often we just don't think about him, and maybe after an event or at the end of the day we think, 'Perhaps he was there' or, 'I wish I'd thought of Jesus—remembered he was with me' or, 'Why wasn't I thinking about him?' or even, 'How could I not have remembered him?'

Prayer for the Christian is meant to infiltrate every moment and every aspect of life, our thoughts and feelings as well as our words and actions. The stepping aside to be alone with Jesus each day is not a self-indulgent practice isolated from the rest of our lives, but is directed at enabling us to live in his presence at each and every moment of our lives. Of course that time of prayer, of being with Jesus, is a vital part of Christian life and discipleship, however short or interrupted or scattered through the day in odd moments. We cannot find God in everyday life without spending that time with him. We go into a time of solitude and silence with God, not for self-indulgence, but so that we can become the people God wants us to be, and to love him and others better.

The difficulty for most of us is realizing that Jesus will actually walk with us from that quiet time of prayer into the ordinary situations of everyday life. Our journey as Christians is in every moment of our lives, and Jesus walks with us whether or not we are aware of him. But we are not always, or perhaps hardly ever, aware of his presence; we may not have succeeded in finding ways to connect Jesus with the incidents of life, of letting him be part of our thoughts and feelings. If only, we might say, if only we had some way of making the connections, of enhancing our awareness of him, and of his life and love being the thread that connects all our thoughts, actions and feelings.

The purpose of these meditations is exactly that—to help you discover the connections, to help you to find ways of being aware of God, of Jesus, in all kinds of situations—in the variety and the ordinariness of daily life, in our daily ups and downs. This is done through meditations which form a kind of rehearsal, a visualizing of God's presence, of the action of Jesus, in a variety of everyday happenings, most of them quite mundane events. Even if you do not find yourself in the situation of a particular meditation, you may find yourself better able to understand and pray for people who are—for example, those with AIDS (now affecting millions in Africa, as well as in other parts of the world).

There is a parallel in the way athletes visualize their performance—that sprint, that pole vault, that high jump. They rehearse the action in their minds, and see themselves performing successfully. Then they are more likely to be successful in doing it. For Christians, it is even more real, because Jesus is truly with us in prayer and in everyday events—transforming the ordinary.

The meditations in this book use events, parables and psalms from the Bible to help bring Jesus into the daily events in our lives, for the Bible is an excellent way of meeting with Jesus, to experience his love and joy and goodness. It is surprising how the actions and words of Jesus in the Gospels can speak to very ordinary situations in our daily lives, however far apart they may appear to be.

We are not superhuman, and we shall still have regrets that we did not recall his presence when we might have done, that we rushed onward without being open to his inner peace and grace and love. But by rehearsing his presence in meditations that help us to find him in everyday events, we are more likely to remember him more often; and sometimes he will surprise and delight us as we find him there—or rather, as he finds us, perhaps in the most unexpected ways.

The more we find him there—genuinely meeting him in ordinary happenings—the more we shall be able to call on his love and grace. It's so easy to get trapped into reacting to situations without calling on his loving guidance. So through these meditations we shall look for his loving grace to support us in pain and grief, in our moods and in difficulties and struggles, to give us patience and forbearance, and to be made aware of his peace. He will also help us to rejoice in his good world, to see the good in the people of his creation, and to celebrate his glory in every aspect of life—to 'look towards him and be bright with joy'.

The meditations can be used by individuals for their own prayer time; they can also be used in groups with one member leading. Below is a guide for those leading a group in discussion and meditation, followed by a guide for you if you are using the meditations on your own.

In these meditations we use God's gift of imagination to bring to our awareness both the Bible event and the linked everyday situation, and to bring the two together. Some also lead into addressing the Lord directly in reflection or in prayer. All of us have this gift of imagination, but some may need a little practice. A sample practice is given after the next section.

LEADING THE DISCUSSION AND MEDITATION IN A GROUP: NOTES FOR LEADERS

PREPARE YOURSELF AND THE GROUP

As leader, you will naturally give time to praying about your role in leading the meditation. It is also vital that you work through the meditation before the group meeting. This will enable you to be sensitive to the pace at which the group can move through it.

The members of the group will gain most from the material if you give some time to explaining the process—discussion, Bible readings, and meditation. A vital part of the preparation will be to discuss the concept of growing to know the presence of Jesus at all times, in all places, and in all moods and feelings. This idea may be completely new to some, while others may have thought about it a great deal; some may have dismissed the idea, while yet others may have worked at it, but become frustrated because they cannot find a way into awareness. People will be helped by knowing that we are all learners. Perhaps most important is the longing, the thirst, to find Jesus.

You can explain the value of being very open in the discussions, being willing to express experiences and feelings, and also to accept, without judgment, the experiences and feelings of others.

When it comes to the pieces from the Bible, the group will appreciate knowing that the passages are retold or paraphrased, mainly to ensure that they can touch us afresh with their message. Note that sometimes there are two or even three linked Bible passages because themes connect different parts of the Bible. You need to explain to the group that the pause after the readings is for reflection, before preparing for the meditation.

The preparation for the meditation is an important process, and you can talk about how you will try to lead the group members into stillness in readiness. You will need to explain that most of the meditations use God's gift of the imagination. There is a strong Christian tradition of using the imagination in prayer, particularly to bring us close to Jesus in the events of the Gospels. Some may find it hard to imagine Gospel scenes, but all have the gift, which can be developed and used. There is an exercise later in this introduction to help people in practising the use of the imagination.

It may be worth reminding the group that we do not have to have a precise picture of Jesus in our imaginations. Some may picture him in biblical dress and style, others in modern dress and manner. But it is perfectly possible to be aware of Jesus in the imagination without actually having a picture of him at all, just as we can be aware of him in prayer.

We all need to remind ourselves—groups and individuals—that the meditations may speak to us in different ways on different occasions, and to various people in various ways. We should also remember that if we do not seem to get something out of a meditation, we have not failed, for God uses time spent with him, and will work in us in his own way.

GROUP FORMATION

If the group members already know one another well and there is an atmosphere of openness and trust, you can skip this section and go on to the next one. However, the discussions may at times need a high level of trust among the group so that people feel confident in expressing their feelings and maybe their failings. So, with a new group, or a group where the members are not yet sufficiently at ease with one another to share this level of trust, the value of the meditations will be enhanced if you invest some time in helping the group to grow together. For example, you can have some sessions of Bible study first, particularly on themes where personal thoughts and feelings can be expressed—and accepted by others. For instance, what thoughts and feeling come into play when reacting to the washing of the disciples' feet (John 13:1–11), the woman at the well (John 4:7–42), or the woman caught in the act of adultery (John 8:2–11)?

You can lead into the meditations gently—perhaps spending more time in the discussions, so that people get used to recounting their own experiences. It might be best to start with meditations which are on common ground ('The supermarket', perhaps), and therefore more familiar and less likely to raise deep emotions.

I. LEADING THE DISCUSSION

The notes on each discussion are there for you to read out, but you may add to them or change them as you wish. Maybe you could read a part and provoke discussion; and then, after initial discussion, move on to more of the written notes. The value of the discussion is that it brings out everyone's experiences, so it will be important to focus on the experiences of *all* the group members. So often, there is a wide and interesting variety of experience, but also many shared thoughts and feelings. Depending on your timetable, you can give the discussion plenty of time, while avoiding too many diversions.

2. THE BIBLE READING

The Bible readings are deliberately retold to try to bring a fresh perspective to them and also to focus on particular aspects of the stories. You may prefer to follow the text of the Bible from a good modern translation such as the New Revised Standard Version (NRSV) —or even, perhaps, *The Bible in Cockney* (Mike Coles, BRF, 2001)! You may find it helpful to allow a pause for silence after the Bible reading so that the group members can reflect on the reading and absorb the content.

3. MOVING INTO STILLNESS

The process of 'moving into stillness' is essential to the quality of the meditation. I find it best to ask people to keep a few moments of silence, to be quite still, to focus on their breathing, and then to think of breathing in the Holy Spirit, and breathing out all that disturbs their inner peace—anxiety, sin, unforgiveness.

4. THE MEDITATION

Once you sense that everyone is fully prepared and still, you can move into the meditation. As most of the meditations use the imagination, the lead-in begins by asking people to 'put a picture in the mind', to imagine the scene. For example, you might say: 'Now imagine the scene… picture yourself in one of those busy, hectic scenes…', thus beginning the meditation on 'Bad hair day'. Other meditations may not require this introduction.

The wording of each meditation is designed to do the work for you. Each line break indicates a pause, and the paragraph breaks a longer pause. In that space, the group members can use their imaginations, or reflect, depending on the particular style of the meditation. You can give plenty of time, being sensitive to the pace at which the group needs to move on.

At the end of the meditation people may welcome a time of silence in which to reflect. You will sense when this is sufficient, and then the closing can be completed with a prayer. The prayer needs to be simple; you will find a suggested prayer at the end of each meditation. If you and the group wish, you can return to the questions raised at the beginning in the Reflection/Discussion.

USING THE IMAGINATION

We are all gifted with wonderful faculties for remembering the past and anticipating the future. Among the remarkable gifts, the visual imagination is particularly powerful. We can put a picture in our minds of scenes from the past, and we can imagine events that we are yet to take part in—like those athletes mentioned earlier.

People differ in the strength of their imagination. Some find word pictures more useful for recalling or looking ahead; and others find more help from their senses and feelings.

Some will say, 'I don't have a very good imagination', meaning that they find it difficult to picture events. Group leaders may find it helpful to discuss this with a group before setting out to use these meditations, perhaps practising the use of imagination first. I have done this exercise with a church congregation in a series of meditations using the imagination during the Sundays in Lent, and they seem to have found that the practice enlivened their use of the imagination.

EXERCISE USING THE IMAGINATION

Ensure that all are settled and in their chairs—it's best to be sitting upright and in a stable position. Then say:

Let's take a few moments to be quite still and calm, leaving aside all that distracts and gets in the way.

Give time for this movement into stillness.

Think of a time when you were really happy, enjoying yourself. It may have been on holiday, a family event, a picnic, a party, making music, a celebration or just a quiet time in the country or at the seaside…

Now imagine the scene—rather like a video. Picture the place. Were you inside or outdoors?

Try to be there again—there in person, not just an observer—there in that place.

If you were outside, can you remember the weather? The setting?
Or if you were inside, the room, its layout, the furnishings?

Picture whatever details you can remember of the place—colours, trees, furniture, decorations.

Now picture the people you were with. Who were they? What were they wearing?
What were their facial expressions? Were they smiling? Laughing?

Can you remember what people were saying? What the atmosphere was like?

Now try to recall your feelings… your happiness, perhaps a sense of fun or just great contentment. Try to feel those emotions now.
Maybe you were smiling, or laughing, or just happily content.

Enjoy the happiness you experienced at that time.
Rest for a moment with those feelings, that sense of happiness and joy.

Finally, let's thank God for that time of joy, for he too was there.

Thank you, Lord, for the happy memories, the times when you gifted us with joy. Help us always to remember you as the giver of all joy. Amen.

FOLLOWING THE READINGS
AND MEDITATIONS ON YOUR OWN

These meditations are equally designed for you to use on your own, though you may find it helpful to read the notes for group leaders. Naturally you will need to give yourself time, and a private place if possible, to work through the reflection, the piece from the Bible, and the meditation.

First, by way of preparation, it would be a good idea to read fairly quickly through the whole of your chosen piece, in order to get a general idea of the theme, and especially so that you can pray, rather than read, the meditation.

The 'reflection' is a time just for that—to reflect on the topic or event, and recall your own and others' experiences. You can think of yourself in the situation, but also use your imagination to think what it is like for other people in their kinds of situations. For example, you may never have driven on a motorway, but you can picture what it might be like for those who do get stuck there—we get plenty of pictures on our TV screens every Bank Holiday weekend.

When you have 'got inside' the event or situation, you can go on to the reading. This is best followed slowly, and with a space for reflection at the end—as befits any reading from the Bible.

The meditations will work best for you if you give yourself plenty of time to let your imagination come alive, but first you need space to move into stillness. You can follow the same pattern as that for group leaders. Sit in an upright, stable position. Try to be quiet and still, focusing on your breathing. Think of breathing in the Holy Spirit, and breathing out all that hinders your peace, all the worries and problems of life.

When you are quite ready, try putting a picture in your mind— having read through the meditation beforehand. Give yourself plenty of time. Pause at each line break to develop the picture and note your feelings. Resist the temptation to read on ahead: remember you are praying rather than reading the meditations. At the end, take time for stillness and reflection. You may like to turn your reflection into a prayer, perhaps simply talking to Jesus about how you feel, what thoughts you have. You could imagine him sitting there with you.

If you find it difficult to use your imagination while reading, you may like to try recording the text on a cassette recorder—with plenty of pauses so that you can simply follow the meditation without having to read.

THE PATTERN OF THE MEDITATIONS

Although this book is a companion volume to my earlier book, which uses meditations from the Gospels (*Step into the Light: Praying the Gospels Creatively*, BRF, 2000), there are some differences. The earlier volume is aimed at helping people to develop a life of prayer that leads to growing their relationship with Jesus. The focus is on bringing to life events in the Gospels so that the praying Christian is able to draw closer to Jesus, to grow from the prayer of talking and asking to the prayer of reflection and listening. Thus the book follows a pattern of development through the three sections, so it is best to work through the meditations from the beginning of the book.

This volume is aimed at bringing events and reflections from the Bible together with everyday life—transforming the ordinary. We look at Jesus in the events of the Gospels, but we then link those events to the ordinary things in our lives. While we hope that this may lead to spiritual growth, the series of meditations does not have a progressive pattern, so you can use the meditations in any order that you feel is appropriate.

MAKING TIME AND SPACE FOR GOD

There is a story of a person who complained after a church service that God had not spoken to him. Faced with the question, 'Have you listened to God at all this week?' he had to admit he had not, and realized that giving time regularly to God to *listen* is the only way to become aware of him *speaking*.

Jesus spent a great deal of time in communion with his heavenly Father—whole nights in prayer. Christians from the earliest days have valued the time of prayer, of being alone with the Lord. We need to make regular time and space—as best we can in our busy lives. Where do we start?

Noise is one of the greatest enemies of our time. Noise is everywhere—trains, traffic, planes, piped music and voices. You will not find God in noise. When God called Elijah to his presence, you might have expected God to be in some powerful, crashing happening. Not so. God was not in the violent wind, nor in the earthquake, nor in the great fire. But 'after the fire a sound of sheer silence' (1 Kings 19:12) and then Elijah hid his face, for he knew the presence of the Lord—in the silence.

Since we are besieged by noise, many of us are afraid of silence. Silence is at the heart of the prayer of the presence of God. We know that Jesus spent time in prayer. 'He had a deep need to be alone, silent and still,' writes Margaret Magdalen (*Jesus, Man of Prayer*, Eagle, 1987, p. 39). Any number of people have been thrilled by the discovery of silence, and we can all, from children upwards, make this discovery. A teacher writes:

When I was head of an inner-urban, multicultural school, I used to worry about assemblies. How could I ask this mix of Buddhists, Muslims, Jews, atheists and a few Christians to pray? It occurred to me that a tradition of silence lay at the back of all our traditions. So that is what we did. Monday assembly was silence... we just sat still... every adult in the school used to come to those assemblies too.
DAVID BARTON WRITING IN *QUIET PLACES*, NEWSLETTER OF THE QUIET GARDEN MOVEMENT

We need to find a time and a place to pray, and we need to find ways into silence. A simple way is to start from an event in the Gospels and, having moved into stillness, imagine yourself to be there. Picture the people and the happenings; try to hear what people are saying. Listen especially to Jesus, and imagine his loving actions—healing, forgiving, teaching, supporting. You may want to say something to him. Sooner or later this will lead you into silence. And you may then find that silence in the presence of the Lord is all you need, simply letting his love enfold you.

There are, of course, many other ways to lead into the prayer of silence. Silence is the key to the prayer of God's presence, learning to sense that presence in ordinary, everyday events.. We can learn to carry that inner stillness, the 'cell of silence', into all our thoughts and feelings and actions. The meditations that follow are intended to help this process of transforming the ordinary. 'Be still and know that I am God' (Psalm 46).

I

BIRTHDAYS

REFLECTION / DISCUSSION

We have all rejoiced at the wonderful, miraculous event of birth. A son or daughter, a grandchild, a nephew or niece. When we and they are young, we look forward eagerly to birthdays, a tremendous excitement gripping us, eager with expectation. We celebrate and enjoy our birthdays, even go overboard with our celebrations.

As we get older, however, that may change to a lower key, a quieter sort of celebration—change, maybe, to indifference or even regret. We lose interest in our birthdays. The 'round figure' birthdays marking the passing decades may bring more sadness than joy.

How do we feel about birthdays now? Do we put on a brave face but inside feel untouched? Have we lost the art of celebrating? Do we instead celebrate too wildly, trying to compensate for the passing years? Or does the birthday simply make us resigned to growing older?

And what about other people's birthdays? We want to celebrate and give surprises, and we hope they will enjoy what we do and respond by being happy. Perhaps they don't want to celebrate either, and would rather keep it all low-key. How do we feel about birthdays?

FROM THE BIBLE

LUKE 2:8–14; JOHN 3:1–16; LUKE 24:1–9

When Jesus was born in Bethlehem, there were some shepherds out in the fields at night, guarding their sheep. Suddenly they were terrified and amazed at the great light of God's glory as an angel of the Lord appeared before them. The angel announced the glorious news that the Saviour had been born in Bethlehem. And while the shepherds were still stunned by the glory and the news, a host of heaven burst upon them singing praises to God: 'Glory to God in the highest heaven,' they sang, 'and on earth peace among those whom he favours!'

Jesus once had a late-night encounter with one of the Pharisees who was trying to find out what lay behind the teaching of Jesus about the kingdom of God. Nicodemus was utterly amazed when Jesus said to him, 'To see the kingdom of God, you must be born again.' The subsequent discussion left Nicodemus with a great deal to think about—indeed, a puzzle, for all his learning. To be born of the Spirit, Jesus had told him, is the way into new life, into the kingdom of heaven.

On the third day after Jesus had been crucified, some women came to the tomb where he was buried in order to complete the burial rituals. To their amazement, they found that the great stone in front of the tomb had been rolled away. When they looked into the tomb, they also found that the body of Jesus was not there. Then they were dazzled and terrified to be greeted by two angels who announced to them that Jesus had risen. Overwhelmed with joy, they rushed off to tell the rest of the disciples. The risen Christ changed all their lives—for ever.

MEDITATION

Imagine that you are a shepherd. It is night, very dark, and cold midwinter. You huddle in your cloak.

You cannot sleep—at least, you can only manage short spells of half-sleep—for there are likely to be wolves prowling around. So you sit, guarding the entrance to your sheep pen.

Occasionally you call out to other shepherds who are not far away. There is comfort in knowing that other people are around.

Suddenly you are terrified, awestruck by the most amazing and dazzling light. Falling to the ground and covering your face, you are further astonished to hear the voice announcing that this is the angel Gabriel, and telling you not to be afraid.

While you still cower in awe, he goes on to announce wonderful news: 'A Saviour is born to you; he is the Christ. You will find him in a stable in Bethlehem, lying in the manger, wrapped in bands of cloth.'

What glorious news! But how can this be? The Christ, the Messiah of God, born in a stable?

Suddenly the angel Gabriel is joined by a vast heavenly host of angels, with even more blazing light, and singing, 'Glory to God in the highest, and peace to all on earth.'

The visit to the stable where the Christ-child was born is something you will never forget. You carry the picture of that scene in your heart throughout your life—the lovely young mother, the beautiful baby, the wonderful sense of peace and joy, the sense of God's love and glory.

Many years later, you find yourself among those who listen to Jesus as he speaks of the love of the heavenly Father and the joy of his kingdom. People flock to hear him and wonder at his power to preach and to heal. How wonderful to have heard the angel announce his birth, and now to see him at work!

You feel committed to him as a lifelong follower.

Then there is a cruel and unjust death; for a time you are lost and shattered.

It is the women, you hear, who brave a visit to the tomb where Jesus is buried. They are perplexed to find he is not there.

Imagine the angels announcing to them that Jesus is risen—a glorious miracle as great, as wonderful and as joyous as his birth.

You and all the followers of Jesus are amazed and thrilled, and filled with joyful new life.

Let's think now of our birthdays. Do they seem unimportant? Would it not be better to let them pass by without any fuss?

But let's pause. Just as there were angels at the birth of Jesus, rejoicing in the news and singing God's praises, was there not an angel at the birth of each one of us? Jesus talked of our angels, our guardian angels,* who see the face of his heavenly Father.

Surely our angels rejoiced at our creation, and sang God's praises, celebrating our birth.

How does my angel celebrate my birthday? Most certainly he sings with joy as he sang at my birth, when I was created in God's image and to reflect God's glory in my life.

What a wonderful thought. Let's pause and reflect on this.

Of course we haven't always reflected his glory—sometimes quite the reverse. There have been some bad moments. Did our angels weep at those bad moments? Were they sad for us?

As Christians we are born again—given new life in Christ.

We are the answer to Nicodemus, born again of water and the Spirit.

Each birthday we celebrate, and our angels celebrate, this new birth, this renewal of our life in Christ. We rejoice in our oneness with Jesus.

We sing God's praises together—my angel and me.

There were angels too at the tomb of the risen Christ. They announced—and then celebrated—his resurrection. The risen Christ lives in us through his Spirit.

One day—a year closer with this birthday—our death will lead us through the resurrection gateway into his glorious presence. Then we shall sing with all the angels of God and they with us, in the wonderful glory of his presence.

So perhaps our birthdays are both a present celebration with our angel of new birth in Christ...

...and also a rehearsal for the ultimate celebration in God's heaven with our angel and all the angels of heaven singing his glory.

Let's be grateful and joyful as we reflect on that, singing in our hearts, with our angels, God's praises and our thanksgiving. Let's celebrate!

✠

Lord, we celebrate with joy your gift of new life, and we rejoice in the gift of another year. We pray that we may so live in Christ, that we look forward with joy to celebrating in the glory of your heavenly kingdom.

* See Matthew 18:10

2

THE SUPERMARKET

REFLECTION / DISCUSSION

Some of us love it and some of us hate it. But we have to do it—go to the supermarket and get the shopping (unless we can afford something different).

You may enjoy the friendly chat, meeting people you know or those you talk to in the checkout queue.

Alternatively, you can get all the way round, and then find you've missed something right at the beginning, and have to go all the way back. You've got a trolley that pulls sideways, and it's very heavy. They've rearranged some of the shelving, and now you can't find what you want. There's always one item (or more) that you just cannot find, and at that moment there's no one to ask. Eventually you find it, or you just give up.

Then there's the queue at the till. You pick the most promising, with only one or two people in front of you. But then the till closes, or the checkout person has to change the till roll, or somebody in front has forgotten something or wants to change an item. And you should have been home ten minutes ago.

What are your experiences of the joys and frustrations of supermarket shopping?

FROM THE BIBLE

MARK 10:13–16

Jesus always attracted crowds around him. They came from far and wide, and of course they all wanted to get near him, to hear him, to touch him, to be healed by him. So the disciples sometimes had a job keeping people back. After all, they wanted to protect Jesus.

One day they just went too far. Some parents wanted to bring their children to Jesus so that he could bless them. But the disciples, being protective perhaps, said, 'No way—you can't push in here.'

But Jesus wasn't having that; in fact, he was quite indignant. 'Let the children come to me,' he said. 'You mustn't stop them. The kingdom of God belongs to children. You need to have a child-like faith to enter the kingdom.' So he took the children in his arms and blessed each one of them.

MEDITATION

Picture yourself in the queue for the till at the supermarket. You need to get home, but there's a trainee on the till, and he's desperately slow. It's a pity you didn't pick the other one; you look across, but it's too late now—there's someone else in that queue. You'll just have to stay where you are.

You look around and see the people, each with a loaded trolley, waiting. Some patiently, some wishing to get on. Some with fractious children, some looking worried and anxious.

You try to look at them through the eyes of Jesus What does he see? How does Jesus see each one of these people?

They are like children—they *are* children; they are God's children. Each one is made in the image of God, made to reflect his glory and his love.

You bring to mind the picture of Jesus and the children who were brought to him for blessing. He takes each one in his arms and blesses them.

Jesus sees all these people in the supermarket. He wants to bless them. He longs for them to come to him—like the children in the Gospel story.

So you look round, and lift each one up to him for him to bless.

A young mother in the next line has her baby sleeping in the trolley. They both look peaceful and contented; God has blessed them.

May he continue to bless them; and you pray that others may share in that blessing.

There's another parent, with a rebellious teenager looking angry, argumentative and uncooperative. He clearly didn't want to come shopping in the first place, but his mother needed a helping hand. She looks tired and frustrated. Life is a struggle.

May God bless and support her; may he bring peace and patience to her teenage son. May we too be considerate to our children and our parents.

The trainee at the till is struggling too. His fingers and his brain aren't working fast enough for his or his supervisor's liking. The pressure is making it more difficult for him. Perhaps he needs the job, but is clearly not enjoying it at this present moment.

May God grant him agility of mind and dexterity of hand to do his job well, and may he find some satisfaction in it. May God grant us patience and understanding, and help us to show appreciation to all in such crucial jobs.

There's an older couple in front, their faces lined with years of care. There's not much in their trolley, and the cheaper brands at that. Life has been hard. Their faces show that, but they also show a serenity and contentment with life and with one another.

May God bless them in the autumn of their lives, and grant them continuation of that peace.

You look across at the tobacco kiosk. Jesus must see this with some sadness—an addiction that is hard to kick, and that brings disease and death to many.

You pray for those who are addicted—for all addicts. May God grant them release. May he heal those who suffer dreadful illness from smoking.

There's dissension at the next till. The assistant is trying to explain to an irritated customer that the vouchers he has cannot be exchanged for goods at this store. She has been well trained, and is patient, gently repeating the point in a different way: she'd like to help, but cannot.

The customer mutters and grumbles. You can't help feeling that the irritation and discontent stem from some deep-seated anxieties or experiences. You pray for both of them. May the Lord look on the woman at the till with his grace, and grant her continuing patience. May he relieve the inner concerns of the customer, and grant understanding.

At last it's your turn. As you pack each bag and load the shopping into the trolley, you thank God for his generosity. So many good things for so many people—what an abundance of good things here for all. May God be praised for his gracious, generous love.

You take a last look at the people around as you wheel your trolley out. All are God's much-loved children. Jesus looks on each one and longs for them to know and rejoice in his love.

✢

Lord, I commit all who shop, and all who serve in shops, to your safe and tender keeping. I pray that each of your children may learn of your love for them and be blessed by you.

3

EXERCISE/SPORT

REFLECTION / DISCUSSION

There are dozens of ways of getting fit and keeping fit—and as many excuses for avoiding doing so. We live in an age when there are fashions for fitness. There's the general term 'aerobic' exercise, with all the fads and fashions of various kinds, such as step aerobics. There are the flexibility and strength exercises, like yoga and Pilates.

Then there's all the paraphernalia in the gym, machines for running and cycling, and weights to lift and work on. Alternatively you can buy home versions and do the workout in your own space.

Of course, you can also go walking or jogging (or both), or cycling. Or you can avoid the boredom of this by getting off the bus or tube one stop earlier and walking the rest of the way, and running upstairs instead of taking the lift.

Many people prefer to do a sport or athletics of some kind, gaining a measure of enjoyment along with their fitness. There are so many to choose, from the gentler way of golf to the tougher contact sports such as rugby and football. There are team sports from cricket and football to hockey and rowing. There's tennis and squash, and the more individual sports, like cycling, swimming and sculling—all of which can be done in company with others. Enjoyable activities other than 'sports' also get you fit, such as the various kinds of dancing. The choice is endless.

So what do you do? And with what level of enthusiasm? Or do you—like so many people—do little or nothing? Perhaps you take some exercise, but only half-heartedly; or maybe you wish you could and just need to get some enthusiasm and motivation going.

FROM THE BIBLE

ROMANS 12:1–2; 1 CORINTHIANS 6:19–20; 9:24–27; LUKE 10:27

Paul is telling us that our bodies are holy, that they are to be offered to God and kept holy as part of our spiritual worship. For, he says, our bodies are temples of the Holy Spirit, a dwelling place for God. We have been bought with a price, so 'glorify God in your body': 'present your bodies as a living sacrifice, holy and acceptable to God, which is your spiritual worship'.

Paul also advises us to rule our bodies, not to be ruled by them. As good athletes training for a race, we should train to win. He urges us to be disciplined so that we are truly servants of the living God, and our bodies are kept holy, in good condition for his service.

Jesus tells us that the most important law of God is to love him, and to do so with our entire being—mind, spirit, soul and strength. This last means to love God with our physical being, our bodies, as part of our total spiritual activity. Loving God is not just a matter of our minds and hearts. We worship him, we love him, with our bodies as part of our total love and worship for him.

MEDITATION

Imagine you are doing whatever it is you do to keep fit, taking an active part in sport or exercise. Picture yourself working at your sport or exercise.

In particular, feel the *rhythm* of the activity.

Whatever you do will have its own rhythm—running, walking, cycling, rowing, gym exercise, and ball games such as hockey, tennis, football, rugby. Each has its own rhythm of play.

Think yourself into the rhythm.

Now feel in the rhythm that the Holy Spirit is empowering every cell, every fibre in your body. He lives within you; he breathes within you; he gives you life; he is the Lord and giver of life.

If you like, feel yourself breathing the Holy Spirit as you exercise your body. He *is* your life. He activates your body in the rhythm of your activity.

As you imagine your activity, feel your body working hard. Maybe you are getting hot, tired, out of breath.

But feel also that the Spirit of God is working in your body to make it holy, sacred for God, a better instrument for the service and worship of God, to give glory to him.

Feel that the Holy Spirit is enlivening every part of your body, every cell and every muscle, and making all of your body holy, sacred for the Lord.

Now as you exercise or do your sport, use the rhythm as an act of praise, giving praise and glory to God.

You can just use the rhythm, or you can use words in time to the rhythm, such as 'Glory to God, glory to God, glory to God in the highest!' or 'Praise the Lord; praise the Lord, O my soul, and all that is within me praise his holy name'.

Just spend a few moments giving glory to God with the rhythm of your body at work.

As you reach the end of your exercise time—both now in your imagination and in your next real-life exercise time—feel your whole body rejoicing in the gift of God's love, the gifts of his Spirit.

Along with the positive sense of being well exercised, you will have an inner sense of well-being, of your body having worked well but also of God's Holy Spirit working in your body to make it holy.

Give thanks to God for that.

Feel your whole being open to his joy. Feel the grace and power and love of God's Spirit enfolding you, ablaze within you; feel your body alive with his love, giving praise and thanks to God.

Father in heaven, we praise you for your wonderful gift to us of our miraculous bodies. We pray that our bodies may be a true dwelling-place for your Holy Spirit, ever worshipping you in holiness.

4

ANXIETY

REFLECTION / DISCUSSION

Anxiety and worry can beset all of us, and there are so many things that can cause us anxiety. First we must learn to set aside those concerns that are not ours, and those worries that are imaginary, and focus only on the real and substantial causes of anxiety.

They can range from problems in work to problems at home, and problems with people—friends and relations. There is work that is mind-bending and seems almost insoluble; work that has gone wrong, and we can't think how to put it right; work with hard or impossible deadlines, and sometimes other people who do not deliver; budgets that don't add up. We may have colleagues who cause us stress, who do not cooperate, who have misjudged us, who do not like what we have decided, or who just want more power and may hope to edge us to one side or even cause us harm.

Then there are money worries—endless concerns about how to make ends meet, to provide what the children need. Perhaps we need money to make costly repairs, or there are bills we have not budgeted for and which will blow a hole in our savings or wipe out our holiday— an income tax demand, an extra-large rise in the community charge, insurance costs, and lots more.

The effects of anxiety and worry are many and various. Stress can cause physical problems—headaches, back pain, breathlessness, sleep-lessness, indigestion, short attention span—and psychological problems such as short temper, irrationality, and being side-tracked instead of facing up to difficulties. Then there can be eating and drinking disorders.

So what are your anxieties? Are you a born worrier? How do you cope with the problems that beset you?

FROM THE BIBLE

JOHN 9:1–38; MATTHEW 6:25–34

The miracles of Jesus told great truths as well as actually healing people. One of his miracles tells of Jesus as the light of the world. Some people brought to him a young man who had been blind from birth. Jesus' followers thought that the man or his parents must have done something wrong and that the blindness was a punishment. Jesus made it quite clear that this was no punishment—God is not like that. The blindness gave an opportunity for Jesus to show that he is the light of the world, that opening blind eyes is like opening blind minds to God's love. So he healed the blind man, much to people's wonder.

Then the Pharisees got to talk to the man—the Pharisees were the rather strict teachers of the Hebrew Law, which had rules about what you could not do on the sabbath. The healing had been done on the sabbath day, so they reckoned that Jesus was a sinner. The man told them quite clearly that Jesus had healed him. The Pharisees disagreed among themselves as to whether Jesus had done wrong to heal him on the sabbath, and some said that the man could not have been blind from birth anyway. But the young man was quite clear that Jesus was from God.

They sent for his parents to question them. However, the parents got frightened—afraid that the Pharisees would ban them from the synagogue, their place of worship. Rather, they told the Pharisees to talk to their son, who was old enough to answer for himself. So the Pharisees did talk to the young man again, and he was quite bold in telling them that Jesus must be good if he had the power to heal. In the end they got angry with the young man, who said again that Jesus must be from God, otherwise he could not have been healed. So it was the young man who was turned out of the synagogue.

Later Jesus found him and revealed himself as the Messiah. The young man responded, 'Lord, I believe', and he worshipped Jesus.

MEDITATION

Imagine that you are one of the parents of a grown-up son. You love him dearly; but sadly, soon after he was born, you discovered that he was blind. There has been no cure.

Bringing him up has been full of anxiety—how to help him to eat, to dress himself, to find his way around the house and later outside around the town—daily worries.

Then there are constant dangers—he might bang into tables and doorways, or get burnt at the fire.

Together you have tried to nurture him, but the world you live in is harsh, and a blind person has little future. So you constantly worry about his future, and your life is a long round of anxiety.

You worry about how he is coping with his life. You are concerned that he can do no useful work and has little to occupy him. You worry particularly when he has gone off on his own or with friends.

Above all, you are fearful for the future. What will happen to him when you are too old to look after him and, worse still, when you die and he is alone?

One day, all that changes. You walk into the town; you know that your son is somewhere around with one of his few friends.

Today is the sabbath. You arrive outside the synagogue. Something is going on there. The person you keep hearing about but have never seen is there on the steps.

He is called Jesus, and some think he is a great prophet, a man from God.

But there's a great argument going on around him. People are talking furiously and discussing things in a very confused manner. The Pharisees seem to be involved.

You ask people what is happening. They tell you that Jesus has just healed a blind man.

Your heart leaps—it could be your son. You feel a burst of excitement and hope—but is this your son? Or is it someone else?

You also feel a shiver of anxiety. There are so many temporary healings, or even pretend healings, and you fear the cruelty of disappointment.

Through the crowds, you suddenly catch a glimpse of your son. He is dancing with excitement and can obviously see—he has been cured. Your heart leaps with joy, and you pray it may be permanent.

Then, to your surprise, a man from the Pharisees tells you they want to talk to you. This makes you nervous: you tend to be wary of them and of their power.

You do go to the Pharisees. They question you—challenge you, in fact. They demand to know: 'Is that your son? Was he born blind? Who opened his eyes? And how?'

You are terrified. These Pharisees have the power to ban you from the synagogue.

You hesitate. You stammer. You demur, and tell them to ask your son for themselves. After all, he's grown up, he's quite capable of answering, and he must know who healed him and how.

You are now in a worse state of anxiety than ever. What will happen to you? And what will happen to your son? Have you dropped him in it by saying the Pharisees should ask him? Have you dodged your responsibility?

It's more of a worry than ever.

Now things seem to happen very fast. You have lost sight of your son. Someone tells you that the Pharisees are questioning him again. Apparently he's being quite straight with them, and they have got cross with him—in fact, they have turned him out of the synagogue.

You are now carrying more worries and anxieties than ever, and you don't seem to be able to see where your son has got to.

Struggling with your anxiety, you frantically start to search around the town for him.

You are about to give up and go home to wait for him, but then at last you see him. He's with a small group of people gathered around Jesus, listening intently to what Jesus is saying.

You come close to hear him, and are at once absorbed and set at ease.

'Do not be anxious,' Jesus says. 'You can't change your height or anything else by being worried about it. Just look at the flowers around you; they don't worry about what to wear, but they do look very fine.

'So come to me,' he says, 'if you are carrying burdens of worry and anxiety; I will refresh you, set you free.'

You admire his wonderful power and assurance; he brings to you a new sense of peace and tranquillity.

Now move back into the present time. Think of all your present worries, all your anxieties; name each one in turn and lay it down at the feet of Jesus. Offer each burden to him with the certainty that he will carry it for you.

When you have put down each anxiety, each burden, at his feet, just stand in front of him and be aware of how he takes the load from you. Allow his peace to refresh you, to enfold you. Feel a new freedom now that Jesus is carrying your burdens for you.

Lord, we lay all our burdens at your feet and ask you to carry them for us. Help us to remember your promise, and grant us your peace in our hearts.

5

JOURNEY TO WORK

REFLECTION / DISCUSSION

Unless they work at home or in a travelling capacity, everyone in employment has to make a journey to work five days (or more) every week for most of the year. Travelling to work has become, for many people, a substantial undertaking. This is particularly true where the place of work is in some large town or city.

The means of travelling vary tremendously. Most people can no longer simply walk to work, or even take a modest cycle ride. Many people travel by car—some driving very long distances. Some catch a bus, some take a train and are within walking distance at either end.

For many more, the journey involves a combination of catching a train (or two) and a bus at either end. Some even travel by boat (on the Thames, for example, or from the Isle of Wight to Portsmouth).

How do you feel about your journey? For some people, it is time wasted, lost from their day—a blank or void that they must put up with. For very many, it is a daily hassle, an obstacle course before they can even get down to the work of the day. For others, the time is an opportunity—to read, to sleep, to catch up on work, to learn, or just to daydream.

FROM THE BIBLE

MATTHEW 6:9–15

One of the most important events for the disciples as they followed Jesus and grew in the Way was when Jesus taught them the importance of prayer, and gave them, as an example, the prayer that has come to be known as the Lord's Prayer.

Each beautiful phrase is a reflection of the life and teaching of Jesus. We may be over-familiar with the words, used to saying them without really thinking about their inner meaning, but try being reflective.

Here is the Lord's Prayer, each phrase taken on its own:

Abba, Father in heaven; your name is holy.

We pray your kingdom to come; your will to be followed here on earth, as it is in the joyous heavenly place of your holy presence.

We pray that you will feed us each day with bread, for the spirit as well as the body.

We plead forgiveness for our sins, as we forgive those who sin against us. Lead us, Lord, away from temptation, and deliver us from the evil one.

We add, because it is part of biblical teaching, *'Yours, Lord, is the kingdom, the power and the glory, for ever and ever.'*

MEDITATION

Imagine you are one of the twelve disciples of Jesus. You can choose who to be—Peter, James, John or Andrew, for example.

As you have grown to know and love Jesus, you have been fascinated by his ability to step into a quiet place and pray to his heavenly Father.

You and the other disciples long to share in this wonderful gift. So one day, you ask Jesus to teach you to pray.

Phrase by phrase, Jesus teaches the prayer you will come to know as the Lord's Prayer. It is a model prayer—simple, beautiful, and addressed to the heavenly Father of whom Jesus speaks.

As a disciple, you will always treasure this prayer, and feel that as you model prayers on it, Jesus is alongside you, praying with you.

You feel it is a special prayer for your Christian journey. Jesus is the Way; he travels with you on your way—which is his way.

Now picture yourself in your own real life, on your daily journey to work. You leave your home each day, and set out by some means of transport, private or public, or on foot.

As you journey, you turn the business of travelling into a journey of prayer; you think of it as part of the Christian Way. Imagine that as you pray, Jesus is alongside you.

Sometimes you have to concentrate on the road, for safety; but in a bus or train, or at the traffic lights, or on foot or on a bike, there are spaces to give to the Lord.

As you journey on the Way, your prayer will be the Lord's Prayer—slowly and thoughtfully, phrase by phrase. Each day of the week you use one phrase for the journey, and then, with Jesus at your side, you reflect on that phrase as you travel.

It is Monday; you pray: 'Abba, Father in heaven; your name is holy...'

I look to you, loving heavenly Father; I am privileged to address you as Jesus does, with the intimate but ever-respectful 'Abba'. You are always close but you are always holy.

Here is another day, another week. As I travel to work, I think of your love. You are the creator of all people. They are your children, made in your image. You love each one. Help me to see every person I meet today in this light, even to convey some of your love to them.

Lord, bless this day and this week, that I may live and work as your servant, and give glory to your holy name.

Tuesday: 'I pray your kingdom to come, your kingly rule in all our hearts, your will to be followed here in your world as in the joyous heavenly place...'

Jesus was obedient to the will of the heavenly Father. In the Gethsemane garden, he came to terms with that obedience.

Lord, help me to accept your loving and generous kingship, and to follow your will. Sometimes decisions at work are hard to make, and hard to make aright. Help me to seek your guidance and your will.

Lord, I offer to you all the decisions I shall make this day.

Wednesday, as I set out on the Christian Way: 'Lord, I pray that each day you will feed me with bread, for the spirit as well as for the body...'

Lord, I am fortunate to have eaten breakfast today. I pray for the many hungry people, both in this country and in many places in your world. May the wealthy countries become more generous to the poor.

Lord, you are my spiritual food, the living bread that came down from heaven.

Lord, I can do nothing without your help. Help me to live and work in your loving grace.

Thursday: 'Lord, forgive us our sins as we forgive those who sin against us. Lead us away from temptation, and deliver us from all that is evil...'

Lord, it is hard for me to be generous to those who sin against me. Yet I need to forgive from the bottom of my heart, for unforgiveness blocks my openness to your love and to your forgiveness.

Lord, only your grace is sufficient to help me in this. Lord, forgive my sins, and keep me clear of temptation—there is so much to tempt me in my life and work. Protect me from all that is evil this day. Help me to be true to you, the only true good.

Friday: 'Yours, Lord, is the kingdom, the power and the glory, for ever and ever...'

Lord, help me to have the beginnings of a vision of your resurrection glory. Help me to see that your glory is present in all people and in all places, however faintly reflected.

It's so easy to forget your presence in the ordinary, everyday world of work.

Keep reminding me that you are always with me, and your power overcomes all evil. I look forward in hope to sharing your eternal glory.

Thank you, Lord, for your ever-present love on my Christian journey. Help me to remember that you are always with me as I travel your Way.

6

ILLNESS AND PAIN

REFLECTION / DISCUSSION

We all suffer from illness or pain at some point in our lives—some minor illnesses, some serious, some even life-threatening. Sadly, people also suffer from long-term illnesses, or diseases that never go away.

We may get headaches, perhaps migraine. Very many suffer back pain from a muscle injury or a slipped disc. Most of us suffer from colds, sore throats, flu, and other so-called minor ailments.

As well as the more serious illnesses, there are broken limbs and the results of accidents of all kinds. People may suffer trauma—wounds, burns and scalds, or 'grievous bodily harm' from attack by criminals.

Perhaps worst of all, there are those permanent conditions—degenerative diseases, paralysis, or major permanent disablement—that leave people out of action and dependent on others for all of their lives.

The list is endless. But how do we react to being ill and in pain? No one likes discomfort of any kind. Some of us are brave, some are able to be very positive; others complain and feel over-sorry for themselves.

What about you?

FROM THE BIBLE

MARK 14:64–65; 15:15–39; 16:9, 12, 14

Jesus was given a really rough time by his captors. When the high priest and the assembly of chief priests and elders had condemned him, the guards took him over and started to beat him.

The following morning he was taken, bound, to Pilate, who could find no fault in him. Unable to find a way out of condemning him, however, Pilate weakly gave in. First he had Jesus flogged—and a Roman flogging was the most terrible thing. Even then, the soldiers continued to torture him: they forced a crown made of thorns on to his head, and hit his head with a rod, cruelly mocking him.

Finally they led him out to crucify him, but he had been so badly beaten up that he had not the strength to carry his cross, as condemned men were forced to do. So they conscripted someone else to carry it.

Then he was nailed to a cross to suffer the most hideous and painful death that could be inflicted.

The worst event ever was also the greatest act of love. Jesus, God made man, gave himself for all humankind.

Out of evil and sin and pain and death, Jesus brought the greatest possible good. He amazed and remade his followers as he rose from the dead. Mary Magdalene met him at the tomb early in the morning; two others met him as they were walking into the country; and later he came to the eleven disciples as they sat at table. Those whose hearts had died found they had come to life again; where hope had ended, new life and vigour came into being. Thus a miraculous and joyful day came to be celebrated for ever.

MEDITATION

Lord, I am ill and I don't like it. I hate the frustration of being below par, of being unable to do all the things I want and need to do. It hurts, it is painful and I can't help grumbling and complaining about it.

Lord, I need the patience I haven't got; it doesn't come easily— helpless, I get frustrated and irritated.

You were helpless on the cross, Lord. I look at you and your suffering. I need your help.

I look at your cross of pain, Lord, and I also look at your dignity, and your silence under your arrest and trial and crucifixion.

How can I be feeling so sorry for myself when I see how you, Jesus, are suffering for me, how you are bearing all our pain and rescuing us from our self-pity?

Lord, I try to align my small pains with your sufferings. I try to feel that the little I have to bear is reflected in your great act of love and saving grace.

I have a headache—perhaps a migraine—and bands of steel are tightening around my head. The pain is ferocious.

I look at you, the crown of thorns pressed down on your head, the fierce spikes pressing into your head. I picture the same crown upon my head, as I think of you. I feel your crown on my head, and I share a little of your pain, as I know you share mine.

My back is aflame—a disc or a muscle has almost immobilized me. I can hardly move; I hardly dare to move, such is the agony; and I am frustrated at being helpless, and wondering where it will all end.

Lord, I think of that terrible flogging by the Roman soldiers. Your back was torn and shredded. I picture myself with you in your agony: my back is bearing a little, but only a little, of the cruel pains of your back. And you are there in the pains of my back.

My lungs, my throat, are painful. It is hard to breathe; I feel very ill. This frightens me, as I seem to choke for lack of breath.

Lord, I think of you nailed to the cross, hardly able to breathe, let alone speak. To say just a few words must be agony beyond human enduring. Help me, Lord, as I try to picture myself sharing just a sliver of that cross you bear, of the searing, gasping pain as you hang dying on the cross.

A stroke or a disease ends in my paralysis. Lord, I cannot move; I rely totally on others to feed and care for me. There is little enough life in my life. What hope have I got, imprisoned in this helpless body?

I look at you pinned to the cross by those murderous nails, unable to move, your life at a low ebb, helpless; but few people seem to care.

Yet you have love and courage to uphold you. I pray that as I share your cross, I may share your love and courage, offering my life as a sacrifice with yours.

Lord, although my body is useless, may my life be a useful one, giving glory to God, and a source of love, compassion and prayer for others.

Lord, in the midst of pain and illness and suffering, I can seldom see towards the end. Yet we know that out of your self-sacrifice, new life and new joy are given to all.

We rejoice in your glorious resurrection from the dead. As we come to trust you and love you, we are given the joy of sharing your new life, of becoming children of God.

✝

Loving Father, help me to know that whatever I suffer is a share in your sacrificial love in Jesus. Help me to live in the joy and hope that spring from Jesus' glorious resurrection.

7

THE CROWDED PLACE

REFLECTION / DISCUSSION

From time to time we find ourselves in crowded places—sometimes in a real crush. The London Underground is a typical example, especially in the rush hour, when thousands of people get jammed into spaces that can hardly contain them. But there are many such crushes. There is the local railway station where people wait to catch a train to work, another crowd crushed together. There's the marketplace, the shopping mall, the high street in the Christmas rush—so busy, we can barely move. Or we might be trying to find our way out of a football stadium or a theatre or cinema, and be mixed up in a vast throng of people.

Some people like crowds; they feel safe in a large group. Some find them painful, particularly if they suffer from claustrophobia.

Our own reactions to crowds may vary. We may be frustrated because we can't get to where we want to go, or irritated at the mass of people who may keep banging into us. We may dislike crowds, or even feel fear, because of the kind of people we see around us in the crowd (perhaps fear of pickpockets); we may be afraid of being crushed.

So how do we see crowds? What are our feelings? What are our reactions when we are in a crowd, and particularly when we are stuck in an almost immovable crush?

FROM THE BIBLE

MARK 6:30–44

Jesus wanted to take his disciples to a quiet place to rest. But Jesus always drew great crowds of people around him, and it wasn't long before many people found out where he had gone and crowded round him.

Jesus had compassion on the people: he saw them as sheep without a shepherd. He spent a great deal of time teaching them about the kingdom of God. Late in the day, his disciples came to him and suggested that it was time to send them off to the nearest towns and villages to find food and shelter.

But no, he wouldn't send them away. Rather, he told his disciples to feed them—much to their dismay. They couldn't begin to find enough money to buy food for such a crowd.

Jesus asked what food they had got. Little enough—five loaves and two small fish. That was enough for Jesus, and he got the disciples to sit everyone down. Then Jesus took the available food, blessed the bread and broke it, giving it to the disciples to distribute, and did the same with the fish. Miraculously there was plenty for everyone—more than enough with quite a lot over.

MEDITATION

Imagine you are one of the twelve disciples of Jesus. Picture yourself with him as he invites you to come away to an out-of-the-way place for some peace and quiet. You love these times of silence and prayer. You are really looking forward to it.

It doesn't happen. Thousands of people find him and crowd around—a real crush. And Jesus, always generous with himself, opens their minds with his teaching. They hang on every word, all day long, drinking it in.

But enough is enough, and you are concerned for him and for them. It's been a long day, and they must be starving hungry, while he needs a break.

So you suggest to him that it's time to send them away to buy themselves food and find shelter.

But to Jesus, the crowds look like sheep without a shepherd. To your amazement—and alarm—he says, 'No, you find some food for them.'

Imagine how you feel at that.

'But how can we?' you ask. 'We haven't got that sort of money.'

So Jesus asks what you have got in the way of bread. Not nearly enough—five loaves and a couple of fish.

Jesus tells you to organize the crowds, to sit them all down. Picture yourself along with the others as you try to get these wayward, milling crowds to settle down, to sit in groups.

At last they seem to be settled. You heave a sigh of relief. But then you wonder what he is going to do. You still have no money and precious little food.

You watch with wonder and amazement as Jesus takes the loaves in his hands. He holds them up and breaks the bread, as he says the traditional blessing; and then he does the same with the fish.

He hands the broken bread and the fish over to you and the others, and tells you to distribute it to the people.

'Well,' you think, 'that won't go very far.' But you do as you are told. You take the little basket and start handing out food. You have perhaps enough for the first ten or so people, at most.

You are staggered and for ever astounded at what happens, for after the first ten have been fed, there is still plenty left; and indeed after the next ten, and the next. In fact, there is food enough and to spare for that whole crowd.

You are open-mouthed at the endless wonder of Jesus, his generous love, his compassion, his power.

You just pause a moment in admiration and awe.

Now change the picture, to see yourself in a modern-day crowd. Imagine yourself in any kind of crowd, probably a crush, and perhaps moving along, but with difficulty, so that you are surrounded by hundreds of people and unable to move ahead as you would like.

What are your feelings? Are you frustrated? Or irritated? Perhaps you are uneasy—afraid, even—or have a feeling of being hemmed in.

Now look at the crowd through the eyes of Jesus. What does he see?

'They are like sheep without a shepherd'. Jesus loves these people. He has compassion on them. He longs to feed them, to share his life, his love with them.

As you worm your way through the crowd, try to imagine that Jesus is there—alongside you and all of those people.

Sense his love outpoured for each one, his compassion as for the biblical crowds.

Sense how Jesus is longing to reach out and bless each person, to hold them in his love.

As you commend each one to the loving care of Jesus, the good Shepherd, thank God for his great love for each person.

✢

Loving Father, thank you for your wonderful love poured out for each of the many people in every crowd; help us to be aware of your love and to pray your blessing on each person around us.

8

FRIENDS WHO NEED ME

REFLECTION / DISCUSSION

True friends are the ones who don't run away when you are down or in trouble. Sometimes we are afraid to approach people who are in need—bereaved, damaged, broken. We are embarrassed because we think we won't know what to say, or they won't want to talk to us. It's so easy to find excuses, to find ways of letting ourselves off the hook.

There is a cost to giving friendship—time, effort, and perhaps stress. People can make demands on us, their needs can put pressure on us, even if they don't ask for any commitment of time and energy. Sometimes we may feel that they ask too much. Then perhaps we feel enough is enough, and we call a halt; or we carry on with a certain level of resentment. Or we're happy to help when the need first arises, but then lose interest as the weeks and months go by.

Friends need us for many different reasons. There are those who have suffered a bereavement. Others are anxious about something; some may feel that their lives are falling apart for all kinds of reasons—job loss, a broken relationship, children, parents, a stressful dilemma, illness, or just sheer loneliness.

If we are gifted with true generosity of spirit, we are glad to be called upon by those who need us, grateful that we have the time, the discernment, the patience, the compassion to help others. We all too easily underrate our gifts of giving ourselves to others—and we all have gifts.

You have friends who need you. How do you share your time and your gifts, and give prayer, telephone time, company, listening to your friends?

FROM THE BIBLE

LUKE 5:17–26; MATTHEW 25:34–40

Jesus was teaching in a very crowded house one day, when some people wanted to bring their friend to him for healing but found they could not get near him. They decided that the only way they could get their friend to Jesus was to lower him down through the roof on his bed. They got up on the roof, made a hole, and, with ropes at each corner of the bed, lowered him right to Jesus' feet.

The first thing Jesus said—for he could see their faith—was, 'Your sins are forgiven.' This offended the religious officials who were there, since only God can forgive sins. But Jesus, who had God's authority, said to the paralysed person, 'Stand up, take up your bed and go to your home.'

To everyone's amazement, he got up, picked up the bedroll, and went on his way, giving glory to God. Everyone watching was filled with awe, and praised God.

Later, Jesus chose a very graphic way to describe how people would be surprised at their heavenly reward. The king in his parable would call people to his side and say that when he was hungry, they had given him food; when he was thirsty, they had given him something to drink; when a stranger, had welcomed him; when naked, had clothed him; and when in prison, had visited him. They were surprised at this, for they had no memory of having done anything for him. Then he would say, 'When you did this for the least member of my family, you did it for me.'

MEDITATION

Imagine that you are one of several friends and carers of someone who is paralysed. (You may find it helpful to give them a name, male or female.) In fact, this person is so incapacitated that most of their needs have to be met by others. They need regular help with feeding and drinking, they need washing, and above all they need company—someone to talk to, someone to hold their hand.

You can picture how you take it in turns to help your paralysed friend. If you can't do your turn, you ask one of the others, and they in turn will ask you.

Now imagine a day when two or three of the group become enthusiastic about taking your friend to a nearby village where a famous healer is preaching. They call on you to join them: four people are needed to carry the bedroll that your friend lies on.

You actually had something else planned for this afternoon, and it would be rather inconvenient to drop that and help with your friend.

You discuss it with your friends. They tell you that Jesus is famous for healing sick people. It's a marvellous opportunity. Their enthusiasm is genuine and infectious, and you are persuaded, and become equally enthusiastic.

But what does the paralysed person want? She is quite scared at first, and not at all sure about the idea. However, you talk it over, and then she too decides that it's an opportunity not to be missed.

So off you all go.

Now picture yourself carrying the person on the bedroll, one at each corner, excited at the possibility of her being healed.

You arrive at the house, where you find Jesus the healer surrounded by a huge crowd. In fact, there are so many people that you can hardly get near the house, let alone carry your friend inside.

You discuss what to do. Should you try to push your way in? Is there a back way? The window is no good—there's a crush of people outside and you couldn't get near.

There's only one thing for it—not easy, but a bold option. You'll have to get on the roof and lower your friend down.

It's quite a challenge. Two of you scramble up on to the roof—fortunately it comes down low—and start to move the roof covering to one side.

Soon you have made a hole large enough, and you are able to lay your hands on some rope, which you tie to the four corners of the bedroll.

Now all four of you are up on the roof. Others kindly help you to lift your friend up while you pull on the ropes.

After a bit of heaving, you manage to get your friend ready on the roof. She's quite jittery: it's not what she expected. You try to reassure her and persuade her to trust you.

You each hold a rope and, together, you lower her gently.
Below, you can see surprised faces upturned, some quite startled, even anxious. And the one who matters—the healer, Jesus—is right in the middle.
He is not surprised but calm, patient, as though he was expecting this person to be lowered to him.

Somehow the crowd makes enough space for the bed and the person on it. She comes gently to rest on the floor in front of Jesus. You are relieved at that, but wonder what will happen now.
Imagine your feelings.

You hear Jesus speak to her: 'Your sins are forgiven.'
There is a gasp of surprise. You and the crowd are quite taken aback, and some church officials who are there mutter and complain.
'Only God can forgive sins,' they say.
Jesus, using the title 'Son of Man', seems to be claiming that authority. 'Who can he be?' you wonder in your heart. And what power can he have?
Will he now heal your friend?

Jesus exerts his power. 'Stand up,' he says to your friend. 'I say to you, stand up and take up your bed and go home.'

There is another gasp from the crowd. She stands up! The one who was paralysed actually stands.

The people are thrilled and full of wonder. 'Praise God,' you hear them say, amazed at what has happened.

And the person who was paralysed is dancing for joy.

As you and the others scramble down from the roof, you are alive with the wonder of it all, sharing the amazement and joy of the crowd.

The most wonderful moment of your life has come through putting aside your own plans to give help to a friend. Beyond your expectations, God has blessed what you and others have done.

Reflect for a moment on the wonder of God's love and his healing power in Jesus. Rejoice in the gifts he gives you and others, of sharing in his love with those who need him.

✝

Loving Father, we thank you for the opportunities to serve Jesus as we care for the needs of others. Help us always to use our gifts in loving you as we care for your children.

9

BAD HAIR DAY

REFLECTION / DISCUSSION

There are days when everything seems to go wrong. We drop things; we break things; we mess things. Nothing works for us. People are in a bad mood and grumble at us for no reason.

There are pressures on us. We are expected to produce results, or we expect a lot of ourselves. But it's all falling apart. We miss targets and deadlines.

Colleagues and bosses are throwing demands at us that we can't fulfil. They're not pleased at all with what we are doing. We don't seem to be able to get things right.

Maybe we're at home. The baby won't stop crying or the children constantly squabble. Perhaps other people—neighbours, family members—are quarrelling or complaining or grumbling. Everyone seems tetchy, getting on one another's nerves.

Can we think of examples of bad days when everything seems to go wrong, and reflect on them or discuss them? Perhaps we can relive some of them, feeling again the irritation, the frustration, the pressures.

FROM THE BIBLE

MATTHEW 14:13–33

It was one of those hot, dusty, busy days for the disciples. Jesus heard that his friend and cousin, John (known as the Baptist), had been killed by Herod. He went off by boat to an out-of-the-way place by himself to rest and to pray in the silence.

But the crowds came hotfoot to find him and demanded attention all day. He spent his day teaching and healing, so the disciples were kept busy—frantically busy, especially when Jesus said the crowds must be fed. They rushed around, sharing out the food he had miraculously produced for them, trying to be fair to all.

At the end of that long, hot day, he packed the disciples off in a boat, dismissed the crowds and went up the mountain to pray, to be alone and in silence.

Still things were no better for the disciples. Their boat was battered by strong winds and waves, struggling on until early next morning. Then, to their astonishment, they saw Jesus walking on the water.

Peter thought he could do the same, and asked Jesus for help. So Jesus called him. All was well at first, but then the wind and waves began to frighten Peter and he started to sink. Jesus immediately reached out his hand, caught him and saved him, and brought him to the boat. Miraculously the weather became calm and still. The disciples were amazed, filled with awe, and they worshipped Jesus who had brought this peace and calm.

MEDITATION

Picture yourself in the middle of one of those busy, hectic scenes you recalled earlier—a day when everything seems to get in a pickle, when it all goes wrong for you.

Perhaps you are at home, maybe you are at work, or maybe you are doing voluntary work—meals on wheels, being a volunteer driver, working in a Citizen's Advice bureau. Picture the place and perhaps the people around you. Imagine the mistakes you are making and the feeling that you just cannot get it right.

People are making demands. There are deadlines to meet; the phone lines are busy; the computer seizes up and you lose all your work. You have a long shopping list and the supermarket is jam-packed; the cooking for the family meal keeps going wrong. Others may be getting on your nerves, winding you up. Maybe people are arguing, complaining or grumbling—or just in some sort of bad mood.

Take time to imagine the feelings that well up in you. Perhaps you feel irritated, distraught, frustrated, at the end of your tether, thoroughly frazzled and, above all, under pressure.

Now switch to the biblical scene. Imagine you are there—you are one of the disciples.

Picture yourself in the middle of that frenetic day with constant demands from all kinds of people, wanting you to attract Jesus' attention for them.

It's a long, hot, dusty day and you are wound up into a tight, nervous bundle. Imagine how you are feeling.

Jesus seems to have worked a miracle to produce food for those people—and there is more work to be done to share it out, to make sure everyone has something to eat.

At the end of the day, you think you are going to have some peace—a gentle row across the lake, a time of calm and reflection.

But the wind and waves blow up—a strong headwind that you have to battle against. You struggle throughout the night and get nowhere.

Then Jesus comes to you. It's a tremendous shock at first. He's doing the impossible, walking on the water.

Imagine how you gasp with surprise, absolutely terrified.

But Jesus reassures you. 'Do not be afraid,' he says, and you begin to feel calmer.

Then there's Peter. He wants to walk on the water too. But the wind and waves are too much for him. You see him—frightened by the wind and the waves—beginning to sink.

You see the strong hand of Jesus stretched out to bring him to safety.

Jesus is right there with you, and he calms the wind and waves. All is tranquil. The wind and waves are still.

But Jesus brings more than outer stillness. He is the Jesus who goes to the quiet places and the mountain to pray, to be in silence— to be alone with his heavenly Father.
Jesus brings the same calm and stillness into your very being— the stillness of the presence of his Father. Feel yourself breathing in that calm, that stillness. Rest for a space in that peace, letting it soak into you.

Now bring the same Jesus into the scene you imagined earlier— the frantic, frustrating, frenetic scene when all goes adrift and the pressure mounts up on you because so much goes wrong.
Allow yourself to stop, and stand quite still. Put everything on hold.

Imagine Jesus as he stretches out his hand to you. Feel his hand holding you fast, stopping you from sinking.
Feel him creating stillness in the midst of chaos. Feel the inner stillness and calm of Jesus breathe into you, driving away the storms of anxiety and disharmony, quieting the irritation, dispelling the pressure.

Let his peace fill your whole being as you breathe it in at each breath—calm, quiet stillness.
Now rest in that inner peace for a space, until you are ready to face the demands of the situation and deal with the pressure, for Jesus is there with you. He creates within you a pool of tranquillity. You can bring his peace to each aspect of the demands on you, as his strong hand reaches out to you and holds you fast.

✝

Lord, in the turmoil of my life and work, stretch out your hand to me and hold me fast. May your stillness and tranquillity overcome all stress and lead me to your peace.

10

I AM RESENTFUL—
SOMEONE'S ATTACKING ME

REFLECTION / DISCUSSION

Throughout our lives we experience other people saying things to us or about us that hurt, and that we resent. In childhood, it may be our teachers or it may be others in our class. Children can be very cruel. Some may be so-called friends; others perhaps dislike us or resent us—they may be bullies, who for some reason speak ill of us, perhaps spreading rumours that are untrue.

As we grow into adulthood, and perhaps through our adult lives, we have similar experiences. Sometimes they are more subtle: people may be snide, saying hurtful things but wrapping them up so that their cruelty is not so obvious to others. Other people attack us directly, find fault with what we do, complain, get angry, and lay blame. Often this will be the boss, but equally it may be colleagues, acquaintances or even family members.

Our reaction can be to hit back, to be defensive. We can build up resentment against the person or the people who speak ill of us or to us, who find fault or blame. In our minds we can develop ways of retaliation. Poison can seep into our being and infect our thoughts and feelings. We can nurture resentment, dislike, thoughts of revenge. Often we can think only of negative ways of referring to those people. Forgiveness may be the last thing in our minds; rather, we would like to get our own back, to hurt the other person, to get one up on them.

What is your experience of these things? How do you deal with such attacks, and the resentment they cause?

FROM THE BIBLE

LUKE 6:27–36; MATTHEW 6:9–15; LUKE 23:33–34

Jesus taught his disciples many surprising things about how to live. The tradition in which they had been brought up taught them to exact vengeance from anyone who attacked them—an eye for an eye. Jesus turned all this on its head. Love your enemies, he told them, and do good to those who hate you; pray for people who are spiteful to you.

Jesus said that we should treat others in the way we would like them to treat us. It's easy, he said, to love those who love you; even sinners can do this. But, he said, we should love our enemies, do good to them and expect nothing in return. Our reward is that we shall be children of God.

When the disciples wanted to know how to pray, and Jesus taught them what we now know as the Lord's Prayer, he included the phrase about forgiving others as we are forgiven: 'Forgive us our sins as we forgive those who sin against us.' He underlined this after the prayer by reminding the disciples that as they (and we) forgive others who hurt us, so our heavenly Father can forgive us our sins against him.

Later, Jesus suffered a most cruel end. He was terribly treated by the Roman soldiers to whom he had been handed over. He was knocked about, flogged, and finally taken out to the cruellest possible death by crucifixion. Even as they hurt him, hammering great nails into his wrists and ankles, so Jesus prayed to his heavenly Father, 'Father, forgive them; they don't know what they are doing.' At the point of extreme humiliation and pain, Jesus, out of the love in his heart, prayed for his enemies.

MEDITATION

Imagine you are a disciple or close follower of Jesus—perhaps one of the women who were close to him, or John, the beloved disciple. Picture yourself journeying around Palestine with him and the other followers.

Think of the times when he would gather you around or perhaps talk to a bigger crowd. You are surprised, amazed by what he teaches.

Through your upbringing, you have laws embedded in your heart—laws that teach you fundamental ways of behaving. For example, you never hit an enemy harder than he hits you, but always exactly the same—'an eye for an eye, a tooth for a tooth, and a life for a life'.

Now Jesus stuns you by telling you that not only should you not exact revenge, you must also actually try to *love* your enemies. You don't hit back at all, but you do good to them; you even pray for them. It's staggering!

Just try to absorb what a difficult and amazing lesson this is. It reverses everything you have been taught to believe.

Jesus prays often to his heavenly Father, and you and the others ask him to teach you to pray. He gives you the most lovely prayer, which also has a bit of a surprise in it: you ask God to forgive your sins—but only as you forgive those who sin against you. Jesus makes it clear that unforgiveness—refusing to forgive others—is a real block to prayer.

The most amazing thing of all comes at the end of his life. All your hopes for the future are dashed when Jesus is handed over to the hated Romans to be tortured and killed. It is a terrible time.

Picture yourself with the others as near to the cross as you dare. The soldiers are hammering cruel nails into the hands and feet of the three men being tortured and killed.

Your heart is breaking for Jesus. The pain must be appalling, for the other two scream in agony. But Jesus demonstrates his teaching and his love, for even at this terrible moment he prays for his enemies: 'Father, forgive them; they don't know what it is they are doing.'

Even in this moment of heartbreak, you are overwhelmed with wonder at his love. Later you will learn that this love of Jesus lives for ever.

Now put a different picture in your mind. Think of a time when someone was attacking you—perhaps being angry or complaining, or saying something hurtful, perhaps spreading untrue rumours about you.

Try to recall the situation. Who was there? What was being said?

What is your reaction? Do you want to get revenge? To defend yourself and attack back?

Do you think bitter or angry thoughts about this person? Do you nurture resentment and hatred?

It's hard to change this. However, try, instead of being angry or bitter, to pray for that person or those people. Even as they speak, pray in your heart for them.

In your prayer, ask God to bless them with his grace and his love, to pour his blessing on them.

You may need to work quite hard at this for a few moments.

If you find this difficult, see yourself again by the cross and hear Jesus pray for his enemies.

Imagine that the person who is hurting you is standing there with you. Again, ask God to bless them and forgive them. Let God's love flow from Jesus through you to the other person.

Let that same love surround you and uphold you and give you peace.

✛

Loving Father, may the love of Jesus support us as we pray for those who hurt us. Help us to see that the love of Jesus is the same for all of us. May his love replace hurt and resentment with grace and peace.

GARDENS AND GARDENING

REFLECTION / DISCUSSION

Gardens in all their many aspects give a vast amount of pleasure to countless people. You may enjoy gardening, but even if you don't have a garden, or perhaps have only a very small one, you can find great joy in visiting the many beautiful gardens and parks open to the public.

Different people may get their pleasure in gardens and gardening from different aspects—vegetables, flowers, shrubs and trees, water gardens and many more.

There can be huge satisfaction in gardening. You may begin with the design and layout of a garden or part of a garden, creating patterns and form and shape. There is the fun of choosing plants, and the planting and nurturing of them. Then, with patience, you see your work gradually come to fruition, perhaps over several years.

There is also great pleasure in the sheer beauty of the many kinds of flowers and shrubs and trees—so much variety and contrast—as well as the reward of producing fine results in flowers and fruit and vegetables.

Of course, there is also hard work in gardening—often very heavy work. The results may look easily won on television programmes, but the soil has to be dug, fed, weeded and watered; there are seeds to plant, weeds to hoe, compost to be made, fruit and vegetables to be harvested, and a thousand other jobs. Plants need plenty of attention. The rewards come at the end. There is endless pleasure in being able to stand back and admire the beauty of a garden.

Most people who garden, or enjoy gardens, find a peacefulness in them—time to think and reflect. Gardens have an atmosphere of their own. Many people find that time in the garden restores balance and makes for a calmness of mind. So how do you feel about gardens and gardening?

FROM THE BIBLE
GENESIS 2:5—3:24; MATTHEW 26:36–46; JOHN 20:1–18

There are two different stories of God's creation in Genesis (1:1—2:4 and 2:5—3:24). The second one places the humans in a garden. These accounts embody marvellous truths: God's world is good, wonderfully good; he has made all things well, with abundant beauty and abundant resources. Humankind is made in God's image, a kind of representative of God to care for his world.

Sadly, humankind lets God down all too often. We have marred the image of God in us; we have not always cared for his world as we should. There is beauty in the truths of these two stories but also sadness.

There is another garden just outside Jerusalem—the garden of Gethsemane. Here Jesus came with his disciples after the Passover supper they had shared. Here he moved away from his disciples and, in human agony, he prayed, 'Abba, Father, for you all things are possible; remove this cup from me; yet not what I will but what you will.'

He gave his will to his heavenly Father in obedience for the salvation of all humankind.

On the Sunday after he was crucified, a third garden witnessed the most marvellous events, for on Mary Magdalene's early morning visit to the tomb, she made the amazing discovery that the great stone sealing the entrance to the tomb had been rolled away. She ran immediately to tell the disciples.

Later, after Peter and John had been and gone, Mary met the Lord, but at first failed to recognize him. Jesus only spoke her name: 'Mary!' And Mary, overjoyed, fell at his feet. The day of desolation had become the most wonderful day ever, the day of resurrection!

MEDITATION

Imagine you are going out into your garden or a garden of your imagination on, say, a May morning. Picture yourself there, as you stand and look, or wander around. You see how plants are growing, what needs doing next; you enjoy the beauty of the fresh flowers. The garden is vibrant with life. Even weeds are growing at an amazing rate.

Now bring to mind the garden of creation. God, in his abundant love, has made all things well. There is marvellous beauty, and there is joy and peace.

The first garden is the most glorious place, outshining all other gardens. We rest for a moment, breathing in its loveliness and tranquillity.

But the beauty is marred by a sadness—the disobedience of humankind. Alas that we despoil God's marvellous creation—both his world and also our own nature.

Alone we can do nothing to right the wrongs we have done. We can only turn to God and seek his forgiveness and his grace.

Back in our own garden, we take out our spade and fork, and start to dig out weeds, and turn the soil over ready to plant. It is heavy work. We pause often to rest and stretch.

The weeds are deep-rooted; they have got a hold—a bit like the sinfulness of humankind. But God loves us; he hears our pleas for forgiveness and grace. And he has come to our world in the person of Jesus Christ.

Now we picture Jesus in the garden of Gethsemane. We see his agony as he faces the prospect of terrible suffering and death. We try to pray with him, to stay alert, awake.

Lord, if only we could do something. We would share your agony, but we are helpless. We cannot repair the wrongs done by humankind; we are unable to restore ourselves to the Father. Only your sacrifice can do that.

We adore you for your generous love; we worship you in your total self-giving. May your love cleanse all that is evil in us and in your world.

Back in our garden, we look with satisfaction at the digging we have done. Now the ground is clean and clear of weeds, ready for fresh planting. We stand back with contentment.

There's another garden fresh with the early morning. People come and go to visit the tomb in that garden. First we see Mary and observe her surprise and alarm to see that the tomb is open—the stone covering it rolled away.

We see Peter and John come running; we watch them looking into the tomb, and see their wonder that it is empty. Then they too leave.

We see Mary return, crying because she believes someone has stolen the body of her Lord.

Then the biggest surprise of all. Jesus the risen Lord is standing there. What joy!

Mary responds to him, thinking he's the gardener; and he says—as only he can say—her name: 'Mary!'

We share her bliss as she falls at his feet. We share the joy of new creation. Jesus has restored the glory of God's image in humankind. He has overcome sin and evil.

The treasure of God's creation, marred in that first garden, has been recreated and revealed in this garden.

Glory and praise be to the risen Lord. Alleluia.

✜

Lord, we thank you for the beauty of your world, and especially for gardens. We pray that we may find the love and peace of Jesus in gardens, and remember the joy of his resurrection.

12

THE NEWS: DISASTER

REFLECTION / DISCUSSION

Our newspapers and televisions bring to us events from around the world. Much of what we read and see and hear is bad news, and all too often it's a disaster. There are earthquakes in Mexico, floods in Bangladesh, famine in Africa, forest fires in Australia; volcanoes erupt, there is homelessness and hunger in every country, many thousands die of AIDS, there are railway disasters, motorway pile-ups, shipping disasters; a football stadium collapses, the London Underground has a terrible fire.

What is our reaction to the disasters and tragedies of the world? Are we inured to the suffering portrayed on our television screens? Are we, as it were, inoculated against horror? Or are we sickened by the terrible things that happen in God's world—the endless suffering?

Where is the help from the wealthy nations, we can ask, and what can we as powerless individuals do to help in such large-scale disasters?

FROM THE BIBLE

MATTHEW 26:47–50, 56; 27:45–54; 28:1–10

There are various disasters in the Bible—flood, earthquake, storms, famine. To the people of Israel, the greatest disaster in the time of Jesus was that that they were overrun and ruled by the Romans. This invasion was a desecration of their land and their holy city of Jerusalem. Yet hope was always kept alive by the promise of a Messiah, the successor to David, who would rule victoriously and release them from the hated occupying power.

So although the officials of the synagogue and the Law did not recognize Jesus, his disciples had great hopes that he would be the one who would fulfil this destiny. Who knows, this may even have motivated Judas to bring events to a crisis point.

But the great disaster for the disciples was the outcome of Judas' betrayal. Jesus was taken prisoner and, unable to face the prospect of being put to death with him, they all ran away.

Disaster did overtake him—and them. He was condemned to death and executed by the most terrible and cruel means available—crucifixion, death by torture used for the lowest slaves and criminals. It was a total disaster from his disciples' point of view, the end of all their hopes and expectations.

Disaster made the disciples run away. Overcome by fear, they hid, frightened for their own lives—fearful that at any moment the same people would come and take them prisoner and condemn them to the same death.

But it wasn't the end. It was the beginning. As he had promised, on the third day Jesus surprised them beyond their wildest dreams; he was back with them and with us all for ever—back in a new and joyous way, bringing never-ending hope to humankind.

MEDITATION

You are reading the newspaper or watching the television news. There has been a terrible, shocking disaster. It may have been a rail crash, an earthquake, or a serious flood—a disaster on a major scale with many victims, people dead or seriously injured. The pictures you see show a scene of devastation.

What is your reaction? Do you feel the pain and shock? What are you saying—to others or to yourself—about the disaster?

How do you feel about the people killed, maimed or buried alive in the rubble? Or about those washed out of their homes by floods, having lost everything?

What about the families who have lost a father or mother, or both—or sons and daughters? Where is God in all this?

Now switch in your imagination to the scene of the crucifixion, standing, perhaps, among the people around the three crosses.

You can see Jesus hanging, suffering on the cross. Look at him as he hangs there for hours, wracked with pain; even more, suffering spiritually the separation from his heavenly Father.

You see his mother tormented on his behalf, torn with grief, but supported, thankfully, by John the beloved disciple, faithful as ever.

You can see some of the other disciples watching from a distance; the rest have run away, helpless in the face of such a catastrophe.

See how even those watching cower in fear and despair.

In the face of this total disaster, they have given up. For them, there is no future, only danger and despair ahead; overwhelmed by the experience, they have surrendered hope.

Look again at Jesus on the cross. As you witness his suffering, at the same time you witness his saving grace and hope at the centre of every disaster.

We who know the resurrection can see that there is more to this scene of despair than meets the eye.

You see Jesus as he suffers with all those who are victims. You know that Jesus also strengthens those who help the victims of disaster. He is there supporting them, giving them hope.

Now switch back to the disaster you were thinking about from the newspaper or the television.

As our hearts bleed for those who suffer, are we overwhelmed by the scale of disaster? Have we too been conquered by the disaster, and given up hope?

We remember that Jesus is there in the midst of this disaster. He is suffering with those who are injured, with those who are torn by the loss of loved ones.

See Jesus as he supports those courageous people who keep on working to help the victims; many others lose interest, give up hope.

As we recall the glory of his resurrection, how he brought joy and new life to his defeated disciples, we see Jesus as he brings hope to those involved in this disaster.

Even in the midst of heartbreaking chaos, broken bodies and broken lives, he brings hope to those seeking out the injured, comforting the bereaved and organizing the many emergency services to help bring order out of chaos.

Lord, we don't find any of this easy; but we believe that when disaster strikes, it need not overwhelm us.

We can lift up to you those who are involved, knowing that Jesus is there, has been there before, will always be there.

We can give generously of prayer and goods, and support those who seek to relieve disaster.

We see that within every disaster there is heroic courage and love displayed by many people.

As our loving Father holds his hand out to us and those who suffer, we reach out to him, knowing that he will hold us and them fast in his love. We rejoice in the new hope bought by Jesus.

✝

Lord, help us to trust you, and never to give up hope. Help us to put each disaster into your loving hands, while giving out of your love in us, in whatever way we can.

13

TRAFFIC JAMS

REFLECTION / DISCUSSION

We have all been in traffic jams, and most of us have experienced being stuck on the motorway. For many people, the motorway traffic jam is the worst experience. Some of us have been in a motorway jam for one or two hours or more. We may have missed a train or a plane, missed a business appointment, been late for a social event or even for a wedding.

It's an infuriating experience, being impossibly stuck with no way out, no escape. We feel frustrated, enraged, and even in despair. We're always in the wrong lane, of course—the other lanes are moving faster than ours, at least until we switch into them. Some of the other motorists don't behave as we think they should; they cheat, they are pushy. We are almost certainly hot and uncomfortable, and lucky if the car doesn't overheat. We don't even know the cause of the traffic jam—it could be an accident, it could be roadworks, a breakdown, or just the sheer volume of traffic.

People stuck in traffic jams tend to feel very strong emotions—at the least, stress; then anger and frustration; and, at the worst, road rage.

Let's reflect on our experiences of traffic queues and motorway horror stories, and recall the feelings that have arisen in us.

FROM THE BIBLE

JOHN 19:16–30

Mary, the mother of Jesus, spent a lot of her life waiting. Like other mothers, she waited the nine months for his arrival, though there was a level of uncertainty about what to expect from this unusual birth, which demanded patience and trust.

Mary was especially blessed by God, with grace—God's active love. The Holy Spirit overshadowed her and she brought Jesus to birth.

When Jesus had grown up, Mary had to wait with yet more uncertainty as he travelled around the country, preaching and healing, often at risk from those who wanted him killed. Many seemed to be jealous of him, or full of self-righteous hatred.

The longest and most terrible wait for Mary was at the foot of the cross. Watching loved ones suffer is always painful. This suffering was painful beyond understanding. She just waited with courage and prayer and devotion.

With her were just a few others—Mary Clopas, Mary Magdalene and John the beloved disciple. To them it seemed the end—the end of hope. It was a long, long, painful wait, with the death of her beloved son the only outcome.

Jesus committed his mother to the care of John, who from that day took her into his own home; and he committed John to the care of his mother, to be like her son.

Before he died, Jesus spoke the words, 'I thirst'—sometimes interpreted as speaking of his longing love for all people. Finally he cried out, 'It is finished!' as he commended himself into his Father's hands. The waiting was over, but the long sadness had begun.

At least until the third day.

MEDITATION

What we know, but the disciples didn't, is that on the cross Jesus was suffering for the whole world. It was an outpouring of love wonderful beyond belief.

Let's use our imagination to be there at the crucifixion, at the foot of the cross.

Picture the scene. The sky is overcast, black. It is the most hideous sight—the three central figures torn and bloody, in terrible pain, their life ebbing painfully away.

A few curious bystanders occasionally mock. Roman soldiers are standing by, indifferent, waiting to get off duty—used, of course, to this kind of torture. It's all in a day's work for them.

But not for Mary and the others. For them it is unbearable suffering and grief, as they stand by, helpless, unable to do anything but wait. They are deep in pain for the pain of the one they love.

Imagine drawing close to Mary at the foot of the cross, waiting with her and the others. We try to feel some of her pain and grief, yet at the same time her God-given courage.

We might be able to share with her some of our hope and joy, knowing that the cross is not the end.

Above all, let's try to sense and learn from God's gifts to her of patience and fortitude, giving her the strength to wait, as she has spent so much of her life waiting. Nothing obvious, no pretension—just quiet, gentle, loving patience, gracious and dignified.

Let's stay there with her for a while, absorbing that sense of patience and dignity, the gifts of God.

Now move to the motorway, the traffic snarl-up. Picture the scene. A thousand engines clatter and sometimes roar. Maybe it's hot and uncomfortable. Feel the heat and the discomfort.

Occasionally there is a little movement, perhaps someone trying to change lanes. Some people are so pushy.

Sense the feelings that beset you—the utter frustration, the anger at what seems endless and needless delay. Why? Why?

Imagine what may happen when we are late, missing that appointment, that meeting, that event, maybe that plane flight... We can only wait and rage in frustration.

As you sit at the wheel of the car, bring to mind Mary at the cross. Try to let something of her quiet patience seep into you. Reflect on God's gift of her gracious, calm dignity.

Wherever we are, we too can be at the foot of the cross, keeping Jesus company with the same love and devotion as Mary, sharing the same God-given gifts of courage and prayerfulness and patience.

Let's allow that loving patience to override our frustration and bring calm and dignity to our waiting—and peace.

Let that loving patience override the noise, the possibility of anger—and let it bring inner stillness, grace, even joy.

Let us sense that God is here with us, as he was with Mary.

Loving Father, breathe into us that same calm patience and dignity with which you gifted Mary. May your gracious presence with us bring us stillness and inner peace.

14

I AM BLESSED:
I LIFT UP MY HEART

REFLECTION / DISCUSSION

There are moments in all our lives—however plain and simple or even tedious—when we feel a sense of great joy and blessing, of overwhelming happiness and contentment. Such moments may be quite unexpected; we suddenly become aware of how wonderfully blessed we are, how much we have to make us thankful.

Such moments may occur when we have our family around us and we are pleased and grateful for them, for their love—brothers and sisters, parents, children, grandparents, grandchildren, nephews and nieces—they can bring such joy and happiness. We relax and feel a great wealth of happiness in their company.

Or it may be a special occasion. You have won a prize and feel rewarded for all your efforts; or you are being given praise for an achievement, the completion of a good piece of work. Perhaps you have performed well at music or sport, and have a sense of great satisfaction and fulfilment.

It may simply be at the end of a happy day—perhaps one of those blissful summer days when you can be outside, when you can't help feeling good, perhaps glowing, because of the warmth of the sun embracing you, and the world around is alive with colour and beauty. Perhaps you have a sense of peace and well-being. You could be on holiday, with time to unwind and reflect on your blessings.

These precious moments may come unexpectedly; and we might say to ourselves, 'I am so happy; I wish this could last for ever.' When are your moments of great happiness and contentment?

FROM THE BIBLE

JOHN 20:1–20

After Jesus was so cruelly executed by the Romans, who were colluding with his enemies, he was buried in the tomb of a friend with as much honour and dignity as could be managed just before the sabbath began.

Early on the day after the sabbath, some women came to the tomb to finish the rituals of anointing.

To their amazement, the stone had been rolled away. Mary Magdalene ran to tell Peter and John, who in turn ran to the tomb. To their very great surprise, they found the tomb empty and, not yet understanding its significance, went back to the other disciples.

Meanwhile, Mary was in tears because she believed that someone had stolen the body. Blinded by her tears, she saw someone whom she took to be the gardener. The man asked her why she was crying; so Mary asked him if he knew where the body was.

Jesus just said her name: 'Mary!'

Her surprise and joy were beyond words. She fell at his feet saying, 'Rabbouni!' which means 'Master'.

Jesus told her not to cling to him, but to go and tell his followers, so she duly went and announced with great joy, 'I have seen the Lord!'

MEDITATION

Imagine that you are Mary Magdalene—a devoted follower of Jesus, to whom you owe so very much. In fact, you owe everything you are to him, for he has renewed your life.

You have been devastated by the cruel end to his life, the treachery that led to his capture, the mockery of a trial, and the torture and crucifixion. You are totally heartbroken, in despair.

After the rather hasty burial on the eve of the sabbath, you get up at first light the morning after the sabbath to complete the burial rituals—a loving duty.

You get to the tomb. Imagine your surprise to find that the great stone at the opening of the tomb has been rolled to one side. How, you wonder, could that have happened?

Perhaps you had better tell the others.

You run back into the town to tell Peter, who, with John, immediately runs to the tomb. When they get there, you are shocked to discover that the body has been taken away. Who could have done such a thing?

You are desperately upset, and in floods of tears—bitter tears. After all that has happened, how can this be?

There are angels in the tomb—a vision, perhaps? You are in such a state that you hardly know what is happening. 'Why are you crying?' one of them asks.

'They have taken away my Lord,' you reply, 'and I do not know where he is'.

As you turn in the doorway, you see someone—the gardener—and he asks the same question: 'Why are you crying?'

Maybe he knows what they have done with the body. 'If you know,' you say, 'tell me where he is.'

The reply is just one word: 'Mary!' That voice—you know that voice. It is the Lord!

You fall at his feet, saying, 'Master!'

What joy this is. He tells you not to hold on to him, but to go on and tell the others that he is risen.

Wonderful joy overwhelms you. What marvellous blessing—to be the first to meet the Lord risen from the dead. It's a moment of sheer delight, which you would like to last for ever.

Now think of a present-day moment of joy and blessing. In your imagination, try to picture yourself in that time of great happiness.

Picture the scene and the people around you as you bask in the wonderful sense of being blessed.

Now bring into that scene the same sense of joy and happiness that you felt as Mary when you met and recognized the risen Christ.

You bring Jesus, the risen Lord, into the present moment of blessedness.

The glorious resurrection of the Lord Jesus comes into our hearts and minds in the earthly and present moment of joy. We think of him here and now—his glorious presence, his wonderful victory over sin and death.

Jesus is real, Jesus is truly alive. He is here sharing this moment of bliss.

How good it is to be alive. How good it is to be here at this time and on this day. How overwhelming the sense of wonder and joy and new life.

Jesus is here and we hear his words, 'Peace be with you.' We let his joy and peace soak into our hearts as we and the risen Christ share this moment of joy and contentment, of uplifted spirits.

✣

Our hearts are full of gladness as we give you thanks and praise, Lord, for your wonderful and generous presence. Glory be to you, O Lord, for all the moments of blessing we experience in your world.

15

DISAPPOINTMENT

REFLECTION / DISCUSSION

Disappointment is largely about how we feel when something we hope for does not happen. We hope to go somewhere, see someone, do something—but it does not happen and we are disappointed. And we can be disappointed in ourselves when we behave irritably, lose our temper, or say something we regret.

There are bigger disappointments. We are disappointed in someone who lets us down; we had expected better things of them. There are people who do not fulfil their promises, who fall short on delivering what everyone expected. There is usually some disappointment expressed in a leader, certainly in any government, and sometimes in the church.

We can be deeply disappointed on our own or someone else's behalf when we fail to achieve something. We or our children, for example, may not have passed an exam we had expected to pass, or it wasn't passed at the expected level. They or we hoped to go to a particular college or university, but were not accepted; or tried for a job that we thought would be just right, but were turned down. That could be a blow to our self-esteem, knocking us back for a time—although sometimes we have unrealistic expectations of ourselves or others.

Disappointment can sap the will, making us negative and cynical. It can lead us to look backwards with expressions of 'If only…'. On the other hand, disappointment can be overcome, and we can use the experience as a springboard, finding new, positive paths to fulfilment.

So what are your big disappointments, the ones that have knocked you back? How have you handled them, or how will you deal with the current ones?

FROM THE BIBLE

JOHN 20:19–29

Jesus did much to prepare his disciples for his death. He told them several times that it would happen, and warned them that they would desert him and be scattered. They thought they understood, but their great hope was still that Jesus, the Messiah, Son of God, would restore Israel to its former greatness and rescue them from the Roman occupying power.

So when Jesus was taken prisoner, tried, and crucified, they scattered. They ran away and deserted him. It was a terrible blow, which they could not understand. To them it seemed the end.

Then in the evening of the first day of the week, they were behind locked doors for fear of the enemies of Jesus, when he came to them and gave them his greeting: 'Peace be with you!' They were overjoyed.

One of them, Thomas, was not there that Sunday evening. When the other disciples told him about Jesus, he did not believe a word of it. He said that he would need proof: he would need to see and touch the marks of the nails and the spear.

So a week later, when Thomas was there, Jesus came among them again. He said to Thomas, 'Put your finger here to my hands; reach your hand out to my side. Don't doubt; only believe.' Thomas was awestruck; he could only profess Jesus as Lord and God.

Jesus pointed out that Thomas had believed because he had seen him face to face. How blessed, then, were those who had not seen Jesus, but who still came to believe.

MEDITATION

Imagine that you are Thomas, disciple of Jesus. You have followed him through many remarkable times over the last three years. You have grown to admire and love him; he is the most marvellous leader and the most inspiring teacher ever. There is no doubt that he is from God and is here to fulfil God's purposes.

When you celebrate the Passover supper together in Jerusalem, Jesus talks about how he will be leaving the world to go to his Father, but that he will return. You get the impression that, although it might be a painful time, all will be well in the end. Perhaps there will be some sort of battle: war is painful, but victory is sweet.

Nothing can prepare you for the terrible events that come upon him and all of you after the supper. The whole thing turns to an appalling nightmare. In fact, since you take cover, like most of the others, you only realize what is happening from a distance.

Over what seems like a lifetime of deepest distress, there is a trial of sorts, much cruelty to Jesus, and finally the horror of crucifixion —the worst kind of ritually contaminating death possible.

This is not what is meant to happen to the Messiah, the Anointed of God. Surely God has a different kind of plan for the Messiah—a victory over the enemies of Israel, a triumph of royal kingship. What has happened is deeply disappointing. It has reversed all your hopes—and everyone else's hopes.

For some days you are in deep despair.

Your sense of despair and disappointment is not improved when the others tell you that they have seen Jesus alive, very much alive. That's not something you can even begin to believe, and you make this clear to the other disciples.

The news makes no difference to your disappointment. You cannot believe he is alive, but in any case he has lost all credibility after being put to that sort of death by those sort of people.

He cannot possibly fulfil the destiny of the Messiah now.

You are disappointed not only in Jesus; you are also disappointed in God, who made all those promises for the Messiah. What has happened to those grand ideas about the restoration of Israel?

You have lost all hope. Maybe after one more meeting with the others, you will go your own way, though where or how, you cannot think.

Now something amazing happens to you. You go one more time to the upper room where you all meet; there you plan to say your farewells.

Suddenly you are amazed to see Jesus. He is right there in the middle of the room.

You are taken aback, astounded. Can it really be him?

Then your disappointment returns. What sort of hope can you have after that sort of death?

He gives you all his greeting—'Peace be with you'—and you realize that it really is Jesus, and he is real flesh and bone—very much alive.

You are completely overwhelmed. You can hardly believe he is real.

Yet he is real. He looks at you, deep into you. He sees right into your heart.

Your cynicism begins to melt away.

Jesus speaks: 'Thomas, here are my hands—put your finger in these nail-marks. Or my side—put your hand into this spear wound. You need not doubt, only believe.'

A blazing light sears your inner being. Disappointment is trans-formed into glorious hope. God's Messiah has changed not Israel, but the world; Jesus has brought joyous new life to everyone.

You can only exclaim to Jesus: 'My Lord and my God!' Your heart is full to bursting.

Jesus says, 'You believe because you have seen me. Those who have not seen me but believe in me are wonderfully blessed.'

How blessed we are when Jesus transforms disappointment into a new kind of hope!

Now come back to the present time, and bring to mind a disappointment—a time when you hoped for something good, yet your hopes were dashed.

Try to recall your feelings—perhaps it is a current disappointment, or one you have lived with for many years.

Perhaps you have felt bitter, even in despair. Perhaps you feel or have felt like Thomas—that all you had hoped for has gone, leaving only despair and cynicism.

Now look at the risen Lord Jesus Christ. He greets you: 'Peace be with you!'

He looks at you; and he looks into you as he looked into Thomas.

Feel how he melts the bitterness and cynicism in you. Feel the warmth of his restoration of hope in you.

Let the grace and love of Jesus lead you to find in him a way forward—perhaps a new pathway that you had not dreamt of, a different pathway that somehow restores and renews you.

It may be that the risen Christ brings to you an outcome that, although not the one you had hoped for, will in the end be the better one.

Let your heart be open to his will.

✢

Lord, I bring to you my disappointments. I bring to you the times when I am bitterly disappointed, and all my hopes seem dashed to the ground. Help me to look to your resurrection hope. Help me, Lord, to put my entire future into your good hands and to trust your good and perfect will.

16

PAINTING AND DECORATING

REFLECTION / DISCUSSION

For many of us, painting and decorating jobs come round regularly. A room needs redecorating, or an outside door or window needs re-painting. More difficult are the stairs and landing. There is work to be done, and we must get down to it.

Some people really enjoy the work, finding great satisfaction in the result of a job well done—the transformation of a room, perhaps. Others just find it a chore, putting it off as long as possible. Then at last they grit their teeth and buckle down to the job, hoping to get it out of the way quickly and with the minimum of effort. We may have preferences: some like hanging wallpaper and get great satisfaction from that; other dislike wallpapering and would much rather paint.

Whatever the job, there is one essential—the preparation. Often this takes more time and effort than the actual painting or wall-papering—rubbing down paintwork or even burning off old paint; filling cracks, and then sanding down; stripping off old wallpaper, perhaps several layers deep, and then preparing the walls for new paper.

It can be frustrating. Just when the job seems complete, we find another bit of bad plaster to repair, or a crack to fill, or an uneven surface to sandpaper. We are often tempted to skimp on the prep-aration, but if we are not careful, the end result will be poor and unsatisfying.

How do you feel about painting and decorating? What are your experiences, good and bad?

FROM THE BIBLE

MATTHEW 7:24–29

Jesus was a brilliant teacher, and he used parables with great effect. Sometimes he retold familiar stories with a new twist, always vivid and to the point.

One tale he told showed how secure people could be, whatever life might throw at them, if they took his words to heart and acted on them.

These people, he said, would be like someone who built their house on a rock, a truly solid and permanent foundation. When storms and floods hit the house, it would stand firm, thanks to that solid foundation. Jesus' words, his love and grace, help us to withstand the storms in our lives.

On the other hand, there were those who heard what Jesus had to say, but would turn aside and refuse to act on his words. They were like someone who built their house on sand, shifting and insecure. Sure enough, when the storms broke and the floods came, that house wouldn't stand a chance. It would just get washed away because it had no secure foundations. Without the grace and love of Jesus, we cannot withstand everything that life can throw at us.

Not surprisingly, those who heard Jesus' teaching were amazed and impressed—because he taught with such great authority. He is indeed the way, the truth and the life—our way, our truth, our life.

MEDITATION

You've got a room to redecorate. Picture yourself in the room as you look around and plan where to start. Perhaps you first have to strip off the old wallpaper. That's quite a job.

You fetch your scraper to work with, and you damp down a section of the wall and start scraping, peeling off sections of the paper.

It's a tedious job; some pieces come off easily, but you have to work hard at getting the tough bits off. How do you feel about it all?

There's a long way to go till you've got it all cleaned off. It's no good trying to stick new paper over such a mess. Then there will be cracks to fill, and ropy bits of plaster to patch.

You pause in your work; you are finding it dispiriting. You really would like to skimp on this tedious business of preparation.

Then you bring into your imagination Jesus' teaching. You hear him tell you about the house built on sand, and how easily it gets washed away when the storms blow up.

How tempting it is to skimp on the things of God that really matter—to build our lives on the easy way, the worldly wealth, the short cuts—and to miss out on what really matters in the teaching of Jesus in the Gospels, which is often much more demanding.

You turn back to the preparation, and you feel how worthwhile it is to be thorough, even though it is hard work. You know that the end result will be worth the effort.

Now, as you work away, you hear Jesus telling you about the true foundations of faith in him. Faith needs to be built on the rock of his grace and love.

Jesus is the true foundation of our lives. He is our way, our truth, our life. Of course, the Christian life can be tough. Jesus never promises an easy ride: a true disciple of Jesus must take up the cross and follow him.

The result is more than worth the effort, for as Christians we are sustained by God's grace. The strength of our life in Christ is like the house built on the rock: it can withstand the battering of whatever storms may come.

You try to keep these wonderful truths in mind as you picture yourself at work on the preparation of the walls.

Maybe, as you wield your scraper, you could be saying in time to the rhythm of your work, 'Jesus is the way… Jesus is my way. Jesus is the truth… Jesus is my truth. Jesus is the life… Jesus is my life.'

Eventually you finish scraping and start filling cracks and holes with plaster. When that is dry, you sandpaper so that your wall is now clean, smooth and well prepared for hanging the new wallpaper.

You step back and reflect: here is a sure foundation. Jesus is my sure foundation.

✟

Thank you, Lord Jesus, for being with me. Thank you for being the sure foundation of my life. Help me, Lord, to hold fast to your truth, to follow your way, to live my life in your life.

17

I'M LOST—IN DARKNESS

REFLECTION / DISCUSSION

There are many reasons why we can feel low, lost and in darkness. Of course, the underlying reason may be medical, in which case we can talk to our GP, who may prescribe some medication.

There might be countless other reasons—perhaps some effort of ours has gone wrong, our plans have come to grief, and that makes us sad. Or one of our loved ones has a problem, and we are unable to help, but can only fret for them.

Other people cause us hurt, wittingly or unwittingly, and perhaps we can't understand why they have acted or spoken in the way they have—and it lowers our spirits.

We can also feel in darkness in our prayer life. We can feel, as many have done before us, that God is absent, that we are deserted, left on our own. Some of the greatest saints, such as Teresa of Avila, talk of 'spiritual suffering'. They experience a time in a tunnel of darkness, with no apparent light at the end.

What is your experience? Have you been, or are you at present, in such a time of darkness, or suffering from low spirits?

FROM THE BIBLE

JOHN 11:1–44

Mary and Martha had a much-loved brother, Lazarus. Jesus was close to all of them and often came to their house. So when Lazarus fell ill, the sisters sent a message to Jesus to come and heal him, expecting him to rush over to them. For various reasons, however, Jesus delayed his arrival. He then told his disciples that Lazarus was, in fact, dead.

As they journeyed to Bethany where Mary and Martha and Lazarus lived, first Martha came to Jesus and said to him, 'Lord, if you had been here, my brother would not have died.'

Jesus took up some words of Martha about the 'resurrection at the last day', and said, 'I am the resurrection and the life. Those who believe in me, though they die, will live, and everyone who lives and believes in me will never die.'

Martha professed her belief in Jesus as Messiah and the Son of God, though it wasn't clear that she really understood what Jesus was saying.

Then Martha called Mary, who rushed out and knelt at Jesus' feet, weeping. She used the same words: 'Lord, if you had been here, my brother would not have died.'

Jesus, too, was deeply moved. In fact, he wept. Then they came to the tomb where Lazarus, now dead for four days, was lying.

Jesus called to Lazarus to come out from the tomb and, to the amazement and wonder of all, Lazarus walked out.

MEDITATION

Imagine that you are Martha, sister of Mary. You live together with your sister and your brother Lazarus, of whom you are very fond, and who is in effect the breadwinner of the family.

You are very close to one another, a very united family.

You are also close to Jesus. He visits you quite often, calling by for a meal or to stay the night. It is the greatest joy and delight to welcome him, and he seems very much part of your family.

One day, a terrible thing happens. Lazarus falls seriously ill. You treat him as best you can, but he loses strength very rapidly and seems to be fading away.

You are in turmoil—worried sick.

There is only one thing to do. You must get a message to Jesus. You know he will be able to heal Lazarus. A friend runs to find Jesus with the urgent message to come and help.

You continue to nurse Lazarus, who is slipping away fast. Surely Jesus will come soon! You wonder what can be delaying him. He must know how desperate the need is.

You begin to despair. In spite of all your efforts, Lazarus gets rapidly worse, and then in the middle of the longest night of your lives, he dies.

You are devastated. Imagine the despair that now overwhelms you and your sister. How could Lazarus, young and strong, die so suddenly?

You feel that you are in a dark hole, with no light, no future.

In this bleak darkness you spend the next few days mourning, and wondering why Jesus could not come to you. You think of the Psalm: 'My God, my God, why have you forsaken me?'

You feel lost, in utter blackness. You have lost all sense of time; you just give yourself up to despair, totally inconsolable.

Then, at last, Jesus comes to see you. You run out to meet him. Maybe he will offer some sort of consolation, rescue you from the depths of darkness.

It is hard not to be reproachful. 'Lord, if you had been here, my brother would not have died.'

Jesus says something that will often be quoted: 'I am the resurrection and the life.' There may, then, be hope at the end of all our lives.

You go back and call Mary. She comes out and kneels down before Jesus, crying bitterly. She says the same words as you: 'Lord, if you had been here, my brother would not have died.'

Jesus too is overcome with emotion. He loved Lazarus dearly. He comes to the tomb where Lazarus has now been for the last few days. But what can he do now?

To your surprise, and everyone's surprise, Jesus cries out in a very loud voice, 'Lazarus, come out!'

What can this be about? Lazarus has been dead for at least four long days now—there's no chance that he can be alive, let alone brought back from the dead.

You can hardly believe what happens next, for there is Lazarus; he is walking out of the tomb, still wrapped in grave clothes. You are all dumbfounded.

After a long moment when everything seems to stand still, the truth comes home to you. He is alive!

You rush to unwrap the grave clothes. Your despair is turned to joy unquenchable. What a reunion this is!

The deepest darkness has become light. You were lost, in the deepest, darkest hole; but now you have been found. Jesus has brought life to you and your family.

How could you ever doubt Jesus? He is light and life, and the source of all hope.

And later he will bring new life to all in his own resurrection.

Now think of a time when you were feeling lost and in darkness. Perhaps you were feeling much as Martha did when Lazarus died. Perhaps you have felt that Jesus has deserted you, while you despair in a deep, dark hole.

Now picture Jesus on the cross. He too feels that God, his heavenly Father, has deserted him as he quotes those words from Psalm 22, which Martha also thought.

'My God, my God, why have you forsaken me?'

Think of the depth of suffering that Jesus experienced on behalf of all of us who suffer from feeling lost and in darkness.

Yet we know that, in spite of how we feel, Jesus will come to us and restore us to joy and peace. He brings new life to us through his resurrection.

Let's reflect for a moment on his resurrection presence with us.

Lord, when darkness closes in on us, help us to remember that resurrection greeting of Jesus, 'Peace be with you'. Help us to remember that Jesus is our light and our life, our resurrection life.

18

GOOD NEWS

REFLECTION / DISCUSSION

The newspapers, television and radio news programmes are so packed with bad news that it sometimes seems as if good news has become a rarity. Those who write the headlines perhaps feel that bad news sells better than good news.

We don't have to think very hard to find plenty of good news, however. There are many heroes and heroines who save people in dramatic situations, all too often unseen and unsung. Lifesaving operations take place, new cures are discovered, democracy replaces oppressive dictatorship, political prisoners are released.

There are many times when we and those around us share good news—a wedding in the family, a new baby, someone returned from a long time away. Maybe a member of our family has passed an exam, got a new job, gained promotion, won a prize, or achieved in sport, music, art or literature.

We love to share good news. Sometimes we can be so excited that we can't wait to tell everyone, bursting out with our news to the first person we see. And we love to hear good news, to share excitement and joy.

Perhaps we forget the good news that surpasses all other—the good news of the gospel. And we remember how the first disciples couldn't wait to share this good news, to tell it out to everyone who would listen. What joy they had!

Let's think about our good news and recall the excitement, the sharing, the joy.

FROM THE BIBLE

LUKE 10:1–9, 17–24

Jesus, having earlier chosen his twelve disciples, now appoints seventy others, and sends them out ahead of him as part of his mission to preach the kingdom of God. He sends them with no supplies—no money, no bag, no sandals. He tells them to rely on those they meet who will support them. When they enter a town, they are to accept what food is given to them, and they are to heal the sick and announce, 'The kingdom of God has come near you.'

Later those seventy disciples return with joy—mission accomplished. Jesus tells them that he has watched Satan 'fall from heaven like a flash of lightning'. The rule of darkness and evil has given way before the rule of God's kingdom, and Jesus rejoices in spirit and praises his heavenly Father.

He tells the disciples how blessed they are because of this experience.

MEDITATION

Imagine that you are one of the followers of Jesus. While you are not as close to him as the Twelve, you have listened to his teaching and seen many marvellous things. You feel you have grown as you have learned from Jesus and drawn closer to him.

You have seen how Jesus has healed sick people, many of them. Each healing is a wonderful sign of God at work.

Jesus' teaching is remarkable. He has taught you much about the kingdom of God, his rule over our hearts. You feel you would willingly follow him anywhere.

One day, this willingness is put to the test. Jesus calls together quite a few of you—about seventy people. He says that he wants you to go out in his name to towns and villages. Your mission is to heal the sick and to announce the coming of God's kingdom.

You find the whole idea quite frightening. It's one thing to talk on his behalf when Jesus is there with you, but to go out on your own... How will you know what to say? What will you do if people reject you?

But you are devoted to serving Jesus, so you make up your mind to go out willingly, though you can't help feeling quite a lot of apprehension.

Jesus appears to be making it even more difficult for you all, however. He tells you that you are to go empty-handed: you will not take money, nor a bag of food, nor spare clothes, nor even sandals on your feet. You really do have to rely on him, as you will have no other support.

Feeling some trepidation, you set out, along with a companion— at least there are two of you in it together. In the name of Christ you enter a village, and try to attract the attention of the people who live there.

What sort of reception will they give you? you wonder. Will they be friendly or hostile?

You announce yourselves to the people who come out to see who you are and what you are doing. 'We have come in the name of Jesus Christ,' you say. 'He has sent us to tell you the good news of God's kingdom of love and to heal the sick as a sign of his love.'

There is a silence. One or two mutter that this is all a load of nonsense. But others say you are welcome. At least they seem prepared to listen.

You talk to them about Jesus, about his love, about his power and how he tells of God's kingdom, the heavenly rule in hearts and minds.

It is such wonderful good news; you feel yourself warming to Jesus even as you tell them about him. You tell them how Jesus has healed many sick people—and indeed has told you to heal in his name.

The villagers talk and discuss with you. Some are warm in their acceptance of your message of the good news; others are doubtful, and some leave the gathering.

Then those who had first welcomed you bring out some sick people—three of them—and they ask you to heal them, as you had said.

This is really testing. You can do nothing but trust in Jesus.

Again with some trepidation you do as he has told you: you lay your hands on each one with prayer, asking that God will heal them in the name of Jesus.

To your amazement and joy, they are made whole—healed in body and mind. This is wonderfully good news. You rejoice and give praise to God, sharing the wonder of his generous love and power.

Then you are taken into a house and given food, and a place to sleep. It has been a marvellous day. You thank God for his love.

So you continue. You meet with occasional hostility, but God continues to bless what you do in the name of Jesus.

After several days, you return as bidden to Jesus, bringing the good news of his mission.

You and others of the group of seventy recount the great things that have been done in the name of Jesus. And he rejoices with you at the good news of your mission. He sees the beginning of the end of the reign of evil in the world—'Satan falling like lightning'.

He praises his heavenly Father, and says how blessed you are to have seen what you have seen.

You are alive with joy at the wonders you have shared in. The love and power of Jesus are such good news.

Now think of a time when you have been blessed with good news—news from family or friends, or success in some way. It may be that you have achieved a good result in an exam or performed well in sport or music or in some other activity.

Recall the sense of joy, perhaps euphoria. You may be 'on a high', walking on air a day or so.

Now bring to that achievement the feelings you experienced as a disciple—a great sense of joy but also a powerful awareness that all that was achieved was in the power and the gift of Jesus.

Think next of some piece of good news which has been reported in the newspapers or on television or by people you know. Rejoice again that God is at work, that his loving purposes have brought about good in his world.

Praise God that, in his love, so much good is achieved in his world. Join with Jesus in giving thanks and praise to his loving heavenly Father.

✣

Lord, we praise you for good news, for all that is gifted to us in your world. Help us to remember that all good comes from you, and give us grateful hearts.

19

BORING WORK

REFLECTION / DISCUSSION

We all have to do work of some kind that we think is boring. If we are fortunate, it is not the staple content of our daily work. The tedious work may be just a part of our day-to-day occupation, but it is rare for any job or occupation to be free of any trace of the downright boring.

Sometimes we are helping another person out—stuffing envelopes, counting money, peeling potatoes. Sometimes we are working in the garden or in the house, and we have a repetitive task to do. We grind away at it, thinking how nice it will be when it is over and done with.

For quite a large number of people, however, all the daily work they do is mainly boring, routine and repetitive. The worst of this kind of work was found on the old-fashioned production lines, where people did one very simple task over and over, all day long. Some of Dickens' novels, such as *Hard Times*, exemplify this. Most of that kind of work is now, thankfully, replaced by programmed machines, but some people still have to do it. There are still production lines; there are still sweatshops where people do menial, repetitive tasks day after day. If you do not see people at work in a factory, think of those who work at the supermarket checkout, or take the money at road tolls, or empty our dustbins, or spend the day photocopying or cleaning offices, shops and factories.

One of the worst aspects of boring, repetitive work is the stifling effect it has on the mind and the emotions, the grinding away of sensitivities. If we are not employed on such work, we must be aware of those who are.

What is your experience of boring work? What work of this kind do you have in your life? And when you do such work, how do you cope with it?

FROM THE BIBLE

LUKE 24:13–35

Two of the followers of Jesus set out to walk from Jerusalem to Emmaus on the Sunday after he was crucified. It was probably a walk they had done many times, so they no doubt found it rather tedious. Jerusalem was alive with rumours and gossip—rumours that people had seen Jesus alive. They could talk of nothing else.

As they walked, a stranger caught up with them and asked what they were talking about, and why they looked so sad. They were so surprised that they stopped in their tracks, saying, 'You must be the only person in Jerusalem who hasn't heard about what has been happening.'

When the stranger asked them to explain, they told him about Jesus of Nazareth. They had hoped so much of Jesus, but the chief priests and others had had him condemned to death and crucified. The two followers explained how some people had been to the tomb and claimed to have seen Jesus alive.

Then the stranger talked them through the scriptures, explaining with inspiring insight how it was that the Messiah, the Christ, had to suffer before conquering death and entering into glory. They were so completely enthralled that before they knew it, they had trodden the familiar road without thinking, and arrived at the place where they were to stay.

When he made as if to go on, they persuaded him to stop and have a meal with them. Before they ate, it was the stranger who took the bread, said the familiar blessing over it and broke it. Then suddenly they recognized Jesus, but he vanished from their sight. And they exclaimed to one another, 'Did not our hearts burn within us as he was speaking?' And they hurried back to Jerusalem to tell the others.

MEDITATION

Think of a time when you were engaged in work that was thoroughly boring and tedious. Picture yourself doing those mindless, repetitive tasks.

Try to recall the emptiness of that work. Can you recall the feelings—perhaps of frustration, of longing for the end of the day, watching the clock as it moves so slowly?

What other feelings do you experience in that work? Let your thoughts and imagination rest on these for a few moments; try to sense them again.

Now switch to the Sunday after the crucifixion of Jesus. Imagine you are one of the two followers of Jesus who are setting out to walk from Jerusalem to Emmaus on that Sunday afternoon.

It is a walk you have done so many times that you could probably fall asleep and still find yourself arriving there. It's a tedious seven miles.

Today, however, you both have your minds full of the rumours that have been flying around. Is it true? you wonder. Could Jesus really be alive? Or were the women imagining it? Round and round your conversation goes, in circles.

Then a stranger catches up with you, and asks you what you were talking about, and why you are looking so sad. You respond in surprise that he seems to know so little about what has been going on in Jerusalem.

He takes the lead, however, and starts explaining the scriptures relating to the Messiah, the Christ. You are amazed and enthralled at the story he tells as he unfolds the meanings behind the scriptures.

Indeed, you are on fire with the joy of it. Yes, the Christ had first to suffer, but then he is raised up in glory. A wonderful revelation!

Every step along that familiar road becomes a step of joy. There is no need to be mentally 'miles away'. You feel more alive than you have ever done.

You are surprised to find that you have arrived at your destination, and you persuade the remarkable stranger to join you for a meal.

At the table, you get another surprise: it is the stranger who takes the bread and breaks it, saying the blessing. Suddenly in those familiar actions, your eyes are opened. It is Jesus!

Now you know why your hearts were burning within you, why every step felt so alive. And now you must repeat all those steps in the opposite direction, and join the others in Jerusalem.

Again, on the return, each step is a step of joy, for the risen Lord is with you in your hearts, sharing each familiar step along the road.

Now move back again to your boring work. Imagine yourself doing each routine task, or each bit of the task.

But now, as you work, picture yourself walking with Jesus—to Emmaus and back. As you do each task, or each bit of a task, picture yourself taking a step with Jesus.

Jesus is at your side, in your heart.

Imagine that he is talking to you—perhaps talking about himself. Feel the rhythm of the steps you are taking with him, each step a step of joy.

Allow the rhythm of each step to take over from the boring task as his presence fills you with vibrant joy. Allow him to talk you through his whole story—beginning with his birth, and through his ministry, the wonderful parables he tells you, and then the crucifixion and his glorious resurrection.

Let each episode in the story soak into you so that it becomes part of the rhythm of your work.

He is the Way, your Way, as you walk together.

Lord, we pray for all who have mindless, boring work in their lives. Please help them and us to walk with Jesus the way of resurrection joy.

20

AIDS

Most of us are blessed in that we are not HIV-positive and do not have AIDS; yet AIDS dominates and decimates parts of our world. There are many who suffer—42 million men, women and children at the time of writing. It is the most terrible scourge, and the suffering takes on cruel forms. The bottom line is that it can come as a death warrant, and that is very hard to live with—hard for the sufferer and hard for friends and relations, leaving families devastated and countless children orphaned.

AIDS can involve much physical suffering from constant illnesses which can be difficult to relieve. On top of all this, the HIV / AIDS sufferer has to bear the biased views and irrational fears of many people. Some perceive the disease as a punishment for some sort of sin. Some treat the sufferer as an outcast, a moral leper. Many are afraid of being close to those who have the disease, frightened of the unknown, of catching something they know little or nothing about.

Above all, there are the mental agonies—perhaps depression, fear, guilt, regret, anger, despair. How do we feel about those millions who suffer from HIV / AIDS? How would we feel if we suffered from AIDS?

FROM THE BIBLE

LUKE 10:29–35; 23:32–43

One of the best-known stories told by Jesus illustrated what it means to love your neighbour. It concerns a man travelling from Jerusalem to Jericho when he was attacked by thieves. They mugged him, stole his belongings and left him at the roadside, almost dead. A priest came by but, when he saw the man, passed by on the other side. In the same way, another official, a Levite, saw him and he too continued on the other side of the road.

However, a foreigner—a Samaritan, considered an outcast—took pity on the injured man. He bandaged his wounds, put him on his own donkey, took him to an inn and cared for him. When he had to go on his way, he left money for the innkeeper to go on looking after the man until he was able to return himself.

When Jesus was crucified, there were two thieves crucified with him. One of them, knowing that he was being punished for what he had done wrong, recognized Jesus as the Christ. He said to him, 'Jesus, remember me when you come into your kingdom', and Jesus replied, 'Truly I tell you, today you will be with me in Paradise.'

MEDITATION

Imagine that, one night, you need to take a short cut down a dark and narrow road in a rough part of town. It's not your favourite area—in fact, it's quite scary—but you have to go that way, so you hurry along.

A sudden shock—you find yourself jumped on by men who have been hiding in a doorway. You are hit about the head and body, and remember nothing for some time—though for how long, you can't tell.

Half-conscious, unable to move, you are dimly aware that you are lying at the roadside. Waves of pain swamp you, and you move in and out of consciousness. You wonder if you will survive.

During one moment of being half-awake, you realize that you have been robbed. All your money has gone, and your new leather jacket has been stripped off you. Dimly you feel disbelief, and then anger, before passing out again.

Then you become aware of footsteps coming along the pavement. Perhaps someone will stop and help you. You try to make a sound, but are too weak. The footsteps come to a halt, and you are hopeful.

Then they start off again, and in despair you pass out once more.

After losing consciousness for a time, you are aware of the sound of a motorbike. It comes to a halt. What next? Another mugger?

But no, you hear a rather rough voice expressing concern. The person seems to have a first aid kit, because he's bandaging some of your wounds.

He must be very strong, because he manages to get you on to the motorbike, and hold you there, semi-conscious, while he sits behind you, starts up and drives away.

Still semi-conscious, you find yourself being lifted again, carried and laid on a bed.

After this, in spite of the pain, you must have fallen into a deep sleep.

When you awake, wondering where you are, a young man comes into the room. He looks a really scary type—unshaven, with battered clothes—not someone you would expect to rescue you. But his expression is kind and you feel safe and grateful.

He gets a doctor to come and sort out your injuries. You seem to be in a pub of sorts. As you lie there, you drift in and out of sleep, but gradually you regain full consciousness.

You have all kinds of reactions—anger at the robbers, fear about your recovery, immense gratitude to the stranger who helps you.

You lost everything in the robbery, but when the stranger has to go, he generously leaves money with the landlord. He promises to come back in a couple of days, and pay anything owing, sort out your affairs with your bank, and get you safely home.

You owe everything to this one stranger—possibly your life; yet you have nothing of your own, and now you depend entirely on him, a total stranger. It is a strange experience!

Now imagine you are a person who has developed AIDS.

You feel just as though you have been mugged. You have that sense of loss and helplessness and a level of anger.

You talk to the crucified Lord: Lord, I just don't believe this is happening to me. It can't be real, it cannot be true.

The whole idea makes me angry. And I'm very scared.

Lord, I am so wasted away that I can hardly summon up the strength to talk to you, let alone complain. My body has lost all zest for life. It's all I can do to eat and drink a little; and the pleasure has long since gone from that.

There's nothing to look forward to—no hope, no cure. Only this dwindling away, this drifting, wasting, gradual sliding away.

It wouldn't be so bad if people were not deserting me. Friends who used to enjoy a good life with me have long since gone away.

I feel as though I am lying at the roadside after being mugged, and people are just passing by on the other side.

Even my relatives have little to do with me if they can possibly help it. Just one or two very dear close friends have supported me.

Perhaps it only needs one person, friend or stranger, to care for me—one good Samaritan.

And you, Lord, are the one person who shares my pain—the one stranger, rejected by so many, who has compassion on me.

I see you on the cross, suffering for all humankind, bearing our sins and our sorrow, and bearing this pain and grief.

I feel myself alongside you, also crucified, racked with pain. I pray to you, Lord, that you will remember me when you come into your kingdom.

While I have not committed any crime, I feel guilt. But like the thief who was crucified with you, I hear your promise: 'You will be with me in Paradise.'

Lord, I lift up to you everyone who suffers from AIDS, and ask you to hold them in your loving, healing hands. I pray for those who search for a cure, and for the millions of families who are losing parents and children. Lord, support them in their agony. Lord, help me to hold fast to you, to trust in your loving compassion. Help me to experience your peace.

21

A FEAST—A CELEBRATION

REFLECTION / DISCUSSION

Throughout our lives we have countless celebrations—parties, house warmings, birthday parties, retirement parties, weddings, family gatherings, welcome-home parties and even perhaps the gathering after the funeral of an aged relative who has gone to be with the Lord. Let's think of some of these occasions, recall the feelings of joy, the reunions with friends and family, the atmosphere of fun and togetherness, the conversations, the humour, the laughter, the memories and reminiscences.

We can too easily forget the good times—during a long and gloomy winter, for example, or when we are extra busy or when we receive bad news. And when we are totally immersed in happy occasions, we can forget to be thankful, to recall just how blessed we are. Too immersed in the party atmosphere, we simply relish the sheer enjoyment of the present moment. And we also forget the gracious presence of our Lord at our feasts and festivities—the unseen but ever-present guest. So let's remember some of the good occasions we have enjoyed, and the feelings of happiness and celebration, and reflect on those times.

FROM THE BIBLE

LUKE 24:36–42

Jesus had a mockery of a trial, and was then tortured and killed by the Romans colluding with the religious leaders. Afterwards, his followers were at the lowest possible ebb. Their outlook could not have been bleaker. Their beloved and wonderfully gifted leader, so full of promise, was no more. They were in terror for their lives, and hid away, not knowing what to do or where to go.

As they cowered, frightened, in a house where they hoped to be safe, Jesus gave them the shock of their lives. He came among them quite suddenly. They were completely overwhelmed, not knowing whether he was real or a ghost. But he gave them the joyful greeting, 'Peace be with you.'

They couldn't believe their eyes or ears, and were torn between belief and fear. So he gave them the greeting again: 'Peace be with you.'

Still they were unsure and bewildered, teetering between wondering delight and abject terror.

So, to convince them that he was real and fully alive, Jesus asked for some food. Then he showed them that he was truly alive by eating the food. At last they were convinced, and were overwhelmed with joy—joy beyond their wildest dreams. The worst time of their lives had become the most glorious.

MEDITATION

Think of a celebration that you really enjoyed. Try to picture the scene, the surroundings, the people around you.

Who were they? What sort of things were you talking about?

Maybe it was summer and you were outside, with the sun shining. Perhaps it was evening, winter time, and you were inside, with lighted candles, a blazing fire and lots of warmth and great friends.

Imagine the atmosphere, the buzz, the liveliness, the laughter, the fun, and especially the feelings of happiness and togetherness.

Think of the talk, the conversation, the happy things shared and the remembering of common events in the past. Just savour all this for a few moments, delighting in the atmosphere and all that it means.

Now, imagine that, quite suddenly, Jesus is there! He's right there with you—in the midst of your celebration.

He is the risen Lord.

⋅Imagine your feelings. Astonishment and surprise, perhaps? A moment of fear, even, and wonderment. Can it be real? Am I dreaming?

Then overpowering joy and glorious delight, which thrills you through and through.

How are the others reacting? Do they share your sense of surprise and joy?

Perhaps you and they still find it hard to believe that Jesus is truly present. Yet he is real and strong, and alive.

Feel the overwhelming love and peace that he brings. He actually says to you all, 'Peace be with you.'

Feel the enhanced sense of happiness and well-being and the totally new dimension his presence creates in the gathering. Perhaps your friends, like you, are transformed by his presence.

Feel how you and the others are lifted in mind and spirit, in a kind of heaven—celebrating, exulting.

Dwell on that for a moment—on the feelings of exhilaration in his presence.

Perhaps you feel you need to say something to Jesus. You may want to tell him what's been happening to you lately.

Maybe you just want to tell him how you feel now. He almost certainly says something to you. Listen to him.

Open your heart to him. Perhaps tell him what a wonderful time you are having; thank him for being there. Ask him to help you remember that he is *always* there.

Bask in the wonderful life he gives to each one of you. And celebrate!

✝

Lord, help us to remember that you are with us at every celebration.May we always be thankful and glad as we rejoice in your presence.

22

I'VE SINNED

REFLECTION / DISCUSSION

At one time or another, we have all had severe regrets about some action taken, or words spoken, or thoughts we have had. Maybe we said something cruel or angry to someone, or we told a lie—perhaps out of fear of the truth. It was an instinctive response to something said, asked or done—and that makes us feel bad, because the instinctive response seems such a giveaway of how we really are. Or maybe we said something *about* someone else; perhaps it was unfair, half-true, or just plain catty.

Perhaps there was a time when we denied being a Christian, when we should have stood up and been counted. We were embarrassed or afraid, and when the question was asked or the opportunity came, it was easier to slide away, to pretend, or even to go along with actions and words that we should have disagreed with.

It may be hard to give examples in discussion of such things. Being open about words or actions of which we are ashamed is not easy. But let's remember that God does forgive us, has already forgiven us, and that he will always love us. Let's discuss what we can, and, if necessary, talk in rather general terms about our own experience. But there is healing in sharing, and reassurance that Jesus loves us even when we have fallen short.

FROM THE BIBLE

LUKE 22:31–34, 54–63; JOHN 21:15–19

Peter was a great one for sticking his neck out. Often he would be the first to rush in and say or do something risky—like walking on the water.

At the supper that Jesus ate with his disciples to celebrate the Passover, he warned his disciples of what was to come, though they didn't really understand. Peter brashly promised to follow Jesus to prison and even death, but Jesus predicted that Peter would deny him three times before the cock crowed the next morning.

Then Jesus was betrayed and taken prisoner. John, who knew a few people, got Peter into the courtyard of the high priest's house, where they hoped to keep an eye on what was happening.

It wasn't long before a servant girl spotted Peter and said that she was sure he'd been with Jesus. Peter said, 'I don't know him.' Soon after, a man saw him and said that he must be one of Jesus' followers. Again, Peter said emphatically, 'I am not.'

An hour or so later, someone else identified Peter by his accent: 'Surely he is one of them; he's a Galilean.' This time Peter was even more insistent: 'I don't know what you are talking about.'

It was at that moment that the cock crowed. Across the courtyard, Jesus looked at Peter, and Peter remembered; he went out and wept bitterly.

After he had risen, Jesus surprised his disciples, filling them with wonderful joy, as he met them several times. On one morning at a breakfast of fresh fish by the lake of Galilee, Jesus spoke to Peter. He asked Peter the same question three times: 'Simon, son of John, do you love me?' Each time Peter answered, 'Yes, Lord, you know that I love you', though after the third time, he felt hurt to be asked again. Jesus promised him responsibility—'Feed my sheep,' he said—and predicted a martyr's death for Peter.

MEDITATION

Imagine you are Peter. You have followed Jesus for three years. You are totally devoted to him. You recognized him as the Christ, the Son of God. And he gave you a new name—Peter the rock, instead of Simon.

You feel you could die for him, although you expect him to be completely victorious in ridding the land of the Romans and restoring the kingdom to Israel.

Now events are moving towards some sort of climax. There is an air of expectancy. Last Sunday Jesus rode triumphantly into Jerusalem. Perhaps now he will declare his kingship, be seated on the throne of his forefather David, and begin the new rule.

The Passover supper seems to be the beginning of all this. He talks, although none of you really understands, of what is to come—danger, serious danger.

But you can face that. 'I'll be with you all the way,' you say. 'I'll follow you to the death.' And you are puzzled, even hurt, by what Jesus replies: 'Before cockcrow, you will have denied knowing me, three times.'

You are completely shattered by what happens next. You are in the quiet of the garden, when an armed crowd arrives—the temple police. They are led by Judas, one of your friends. What a betrayal!

Jesus puts up no resistance and is led away. Something has gone dreadfully wrong. Surely he could call upon the heavenly powers to conquer his enemies? Why has he just given in like that? Fear grips you.

John is tugging at your sleeve; you go with him into the town, to the high priest's house and into the courtyard.

Now you really are frightened. These temple police are up to no good. You almost wish you weren't there at all.

One of the women, a serving girl, looks at you suspiciously. 'Aren't you with Jesus?' she asks. Instinctively you blurt out, 'No—I don't even know him.'

Phew, that was close.

But a man comes by and looks at you very curiously. 'You're one of his followers, aren't you?' he asks. 'No, I am not,' you say, quite strongly.

This is getting very uncomfortable. You keep to a dark corner for a long time, but it's cold. That just-before-dawn chill is creeping into you. So you shuffle closer to the fire.

'You're from Galilee,' a voice says close behind you, making you jump. 'You must be one of his.'

Terrified, you stammer, 'I... I don't know what you're talking about.'

Just at that moment, the first cock crows.

And right across the courtyard, Jesus—Jesus is turning towards you, and you glimpse him looking at you.

It's the worst moment of your life. Blinded by tears, you dash into the cold empty street.

How could you have done that? How could you have let him down?

In the trial and the death that follow, your world comes to an end. The dream has died; hope has vanished. Yours was a shameful farewell to the one who was truth and goodness. What is there left to live for?

Imagine the miserable time you are having, for what seems an endless night.

On Sunday morning, though, you hear reports that Jesus is no longer in the tomb where he was laid.

You find it a lot to take in, but more is to come. That evening, you are all together, still terrified of the temple police.

And then—*Jesus is there*! Truly there and very much alive. You are overwhelmed with joy and wonder.

The days that follow are like a dream. You are all new people, living in joy.

But inside you there is a worm of discomfort. How could you have let him down?

You decide it would be a good distraction to go back to fishing, but after a whole night of fishing, there's not much to show for it.

In the morning, you see a man on the shore telling you to cast your net on the other side of the boat. You cast the net, and you get a huge catch, a net full of large fish.

You know that it's Jesus. It can only be Jesus.

You immediately get out of the boat and wade ashore, and there you find that he's already got breakfast for you—baked fish and warm bread.

Then the questions come.

'Simon Peter, do you love me?' He's looking deep into you. And you feel uncomfortable.

'Yes, Lord,' you say, 'you know that I love you.'

'Feed my sheep,' he says.

Again he looks into your eyes, sees right through you. You find it most disturbing. 'Simon Peter, do you love me?'

This is hurting. 'Yes, Lord, you know that I love you.'

'Feed my lambs,' he says again.

He asks a third time, and you feel deeply hurt. 'Simon Peter, do you love me?'

Help! What can you say? 'Lord, you know everything, you know that I love you.'

Again he says, 'Feed my sheep,' and he goes on to predict a tough future for you.

You look at Jesus, and you see clearly what is in his eyes.

You see that in his eyes is not accusation, but love—and forgiveness.

He understands both your betrayal and your terrible sense of shame.

He is restoring you to wholeness and oneness with him.

You feel not only fully forgiven, but renewed, at peace, made whole. You rest in that feeling, basking in God's loving forgiveness.

Lord, all too often I sin and let you down. Lord, forgive me, renew me, and support me with your saving grace.

23

ENTERTAINMENT

REFLECTION / DISCUSSION

It's such a big business today, the world of entertainment. We are besieged with advertisements demanding that we allow a new film or a television show to entertain us—or a theme park, a stately home, a holiday resort.

Entertainment implies that we who are being entertained remain more or less inactive; the entertainers do the work. So it's different from active recreation. Being entertained is a form of relaxation and thus an important element in our lives.

We may find that we have to keep it in balance—entertainment can take us over, and of course we can just become couch potatoes! There may also be a moral element in entertainment: we should be concerned to find the limits to, for example, the viewing of sex and violence. Some forms of entertainment may gain too strong a hold over us, such as gambling or certain computer games.

How and where do you and your family and friends find entertainment? It may be television or videos or computer games; it may be cinema or theatre; it may be the pub, watching live sport, going to the races; or it could be an 'easy-reading' book, or talking with friends. How do you manage to balance and keep control over your entertainment?

FROM THE BIBLE
JOHN 2:1–11; LUKE 21:29–36

Jesus was great at parties. He could be the life and soul of the celebration, so much so that his enemies labelled him 'a glutton and a drunkard'.

Once, there was a wedding of some friends of his mother's, and the bride and groom invited Jesus—and his friends—to join the party. Of course, that meant quite a crowd because he had at least twelve friends, and there came a point when the refreshments started to run out. Most embarrassing! Mary the mother of Jesus asked for his help.

Jesus was reluctant—saying that it was not yet the time to reveal his power. But Mary had great faith in him and told the servants to obey him. When he had told the servants at the feast what to do, sure enough, there was new wine in plenty.

The 'president' of the feast (a kind of chairman and toastmaster) was most impressed with the new wine, and there is little doubt that they all had a very good time indeed—thanks to Jesus.

Over time, Jesus made it clear that being a disciple was never going to be all fun and games. There would be a very serious side, and his followers had to be ready to serve him, open to doing his bidding, at any time. He told many parables to illustrate this. One of his parables of the kingdom used the idea of leaves breaking out on the trees to tell us that summer is on the way. So, too, we must be ready and awake for the kingdom of God—'not weighed down,' Jesus said, 'with dissipation and drunkenness and the worries of this life'. So, entertainment should be kept in its proper place: we need to be alive to the things of God and never let him be crowded out.

MEDITATION

Imagine that you are one of the disciples of Jesus. You have an exhilarating time following him, learning from him and enjoying his company.

Now it's party time—and Jesus is great at parties. This one's a wedding: you are going to join the wedding feast, and that's usually quite some celebration. Some friends of Jesus' mother have invited you and the others. You are very touched that you should all be included.

Imagine that you and the others have got your best clothes on, and come together at the feast. Picture the lively crowd, buzzing with happy conversation and good humour.

You are beginning to enjoy yourselves immensely. The party is going with a swing, just full of fizz.

As the party goes on, however, you begin to sense a change in the atmosphere—a different key. Somehow, the fizz has gone out of it. People are sounding less than full of celebration, even a little disgruntled. Many are holding empty wine cups in their hands and looking around, but the servants are holding empty jugs and looking embarrassed.

Imagine how you feel for the host, not to mention the other guests. A bad party is never lived down, and a wedding party going wrong like this is unheard of.

Mary, Jesus' mother, is the one who is taking the initiative. She is asking Jesus to come to the rescue. He seems to hold back at first, but Mary appears to have every faith in him.

Sure enough, he gives orders to the servants, and suddenly you see them looking more cheerful. In fact, they've really perked up. They dip their empty jugs into what were water jars, and now they are pouring fresh wine into everyone's wine cups. Amazing!

And does it taste good! The bridegroom looks very relieved, as people congratulate him and the party continues with a tremendous swing—thanks to Jesus.

But you and the others feel a deeper joy because Jesus is there. It's difficult to explain, but he makes all the difference. It's not just entertainment, though it is entertaining. Jesus adds a different dimension.

As you continue to follow Jesus, you won't forget that miracle and its significance. Jesus continues to teach you the ways of God, by his life as much as by his words. You know it won't always be party time—Jesus makes that clear. You will need to learn how to keep a balance in your life.

Now bring yourself back into today's world. You have some spare time in which to relax. You can relax with some entertainment.

Choose your entertainment: what would you would most like to be doing?

Imagine, then, that you are relaxed and involved in your favourite entertainment, probably sitting somewhere very comfortably. You may be at the cinema, in a theatre, in a football stadium, in front of the television watching your favourite programme, or you may be immersed in a thriller or a romance.

Just relax into that for a moment, and try to imagine the feelings that come to you when you are being entertained—perhaps laughter, perhaps intense emotions because you are involved in the plot, or fascination, or tension because the characters are in crisis.

Now bring Jesus into the entertainment, sitting alongside you. Imagine how he is—rather as you pictured him at the wedding feast where he rescued the party.

What difference is he making? How do you feel about his presence?

How does he seem to feel about your entertainment? And do you feel differently about the nature of the entertainment now that Jesus is there?

Do you want to say something to him about your entertainment? Perhaps you want to thank him, and ask him to bless what you are doing.

Perhaps you feel challenged by Jesus, uncomfortable about the nature of the entertainment.

Tell Jesus about your feelings, and let his presence guide you. Be glad for his presence with you.

Lord, we thank you for the gift of entertainment, for relaxation and laughter. We pray that our entertainment may always be acceptable to you, that we may keep to the integrity that you taught your disciples.

24

MY DAILY WORK

REFLECTION / DISCUSSION

Attitudes to daily work vary a great deal, and may depend upon whether the work is at home or elsewhere, on whether it is paid or voluntary. Certainly a lot of people's attitudes are summed up in the phrase 'that Monday morning feeling'—the feeling that work is always unpleasant, while leisure and home and family are much more desirable.

Much depends upon the nature of your work. Some people love their work, give vast amounts of time to it, and may even become so-called 'workaholics'.

Others have mixed feelings and enjoy only some parts of their job. We have many daily tasks to do at work or at home, some of which we find tedious, and some of which we just don't like doing at all. Sometimes we grit our teeth and plough on, and sometimes we feel resentful: 'Why should I have to do this?'

Feelings about work also depend upon the other people at work. We may not get on particularly well with them, may not have too much in common with them, may feel they don't pull their weight. Feelings about working may be negative or mixed, however much we like the actual content of the job. Or we may find that we really like the company of those we work with, and therefore enjoy being at work and have plenty of good social interaction, even if the job itself isn't up to much.

Again, our feelings about work may depend upon the kind of boss we have. Do they appreciate what we do, and show it? Or are they unappreciative and perhaps given to finding fault? Do we feel that we are well supported, or do we feel exploited?

FROM THE BIBLE

LUKE 10:38–42

Jesus made many friends—he was that sort of person. People loved him and loved to be with him, to welcome him into their home if the opportunity arose. So it was with the two sisters, Mary and Martha, and their brother, Lazarus. Jesus would stay with them when he could and would certainly join them for a meal if he was passing.

One day, when Jesus visited them, Martha was preparing the meal, and she got quite wound up about the amount she had to do. She was particularly mad at Mary, who was just sitting with Jesus and listening to him.

Eventually the pressure of work got to her and she complained to Jesus, asking him to tell her sister to come and do her share. And Martha and Mary *both* got a surprise.

Jesus didn't tell Mary to go and help Martha. He said to Martha, 'You are fretting and worrying about all your work, but there is only one essential, and that is what Mary has chosen.'

MEDITATION

Picture someone who is very practical, who runs a busy household, is hard-working and sometimes short-tempered, always on the go, always busy.

Now listen to her telling you her story. Use your imagination to picture her at her daily work as she recounts some events in her life and the household where she lives and works.

My name is Martha. I'm the practical one in the family. Not that Mary and Lazarus are lazy and don't do any work—far from it.

It's just that I'm the one who is organized, who gets on and does things. If I didn't take the lead and set to, nothing would ever get done.

It's not because they find many of the household tasks un-interesting. We all do; there's much that we just do not enjoy doing.

But they tend to focus on other things. They prefer just to sit around and talk all day—high-level discussion and no doubt very important, but up in the clouds, not in the least bit practical.

So when Jesus comes by for a meal, it's me who has to get on and do the preparation. Mary just loves to sit at his feet and listen and listen and listen, while I rush around and get the meal, and do all the tasks—interesting or tedious—so that we can sit down together and eat.

Sometimes I feel she should pull her weight in the kitchen, rather than just sitting around. It can be irritating.

Well, one day, it did get too much. Perhaps I was too ambitious in the choice of menu. Jesus was more than happy with very simple food. He never expected anything fancy. But he is so special and I wanted to produce a really special meal for him. I really enjoy doing that.

As I said, it all got too much. There was so much to do, so many vegetables to peel and chop, so many pots on the boil, and the fire getting low and needing attention. All very tedious, perhaps, but it was getting out of hand—and I didn't see why Mary should have the enjoyable business of sitting down and listening to Jesus, while I did the ordinary menial tasks like getting the meal ready.

In the end, I boiled over, and I called out to Jesus and (a bit sarcastically) said, 'Don't you care that my sister isn't helping me?' I was expecting, of course, that he would tell her to lend a hand.

The amazing thing was that he didn't say to her, 'Come on, Mary, pull your weight. Give Martha a hand.'

Instead he said to *me*, 'Martha, you're just getting hot and bothered and fretting quite unnecessarily. Mary has chosen the best part, and that will never be taken away from her.'

Whew! That really stopped me in my tracks. There was I, thinking that all the work I was doing was going to earn some sort of reward, but I'd got it the wrong way round. The work isn't a way of earning rewards; it's our role to be servants to others.

Later, Jesus acted this out—his friend Andrew told me about it. Jesus put a towel around himself and went round washing their feet—all twelve of them! It was a way of showing how if he, the Master, could serve them, they must be more than ready to be servants to others.

Now I do my work quite differently. I'm less resentful about the boring bits. I try to do each task for others. As I peel each vegetable or break an egg, or bake something, or make some soup, I think of the people who will eat. I think them into the Lord's presence. It's the same when I do some service for the others—I try to think of the person it's for.

When I cut up meat or fish, I think also of the shepherd, the herdsman or the fisherman who harvested them. And especially when I hang up washing, I think of the towel that Jesus put around himself to wash his disciples' feet.

Others have told me how the vessels we use for cooking or eating can be treated as if they were sacred—as sacred as those we now use to remember the Lord, to recall his presence at his table when we celebrate his resurrection on the first day of the week. So as I wash the plates and the cooking pots, I try to treat them as sacred. I try to remember that all God's created things are sacred.

He is there; he is always there. His loving, tender presence brings healing and stillness to my inner being—like the way Mary is at the Lord's feet, listening. Only, I am doing it as I work, knowing his presence with me at all times.

Now and again I just stop quite still—a moment of complete silence. He is here.

I think about him, and I listen—being still with him in his presence. That's bliss. That is blessing.

Thank you, Lord, for your presence in everyday things. Help me to find you in my work, whatever the task—to know your loving presence.

25

SOMEONE I LOVE
IS SUFFERING

REFLECTION / DISCUSSION

One of the hardest things to bear in life is the suffering of someone we love. We feel great pain for them, and we feel distress because of our helplessness. We would rather suffer ourselves than stand by, helpless, and watch someone we love suffering. Even worse is to be far away from that loved one. Distance prevents us from being with them, and we long to be near enough to comfort them in some way and support them, to hold them and to uphold them.

All sorts of emotions come to the fore—grief and pain for the one we love. Then there's anger—we can get angry that this should happen, and very angry with God that he should let it happen. How *could* he? Of all people, how could he let this one suffer in this way?

Through it all, our own pain for the loved one simmers and burns within us, together with the endless worry, and the fear—fear of what could happen, what unknown ills may yet occur.

Then we feel we have to remain strong and positive, and that's hard. Our groans and tears are no help to the one suffering; in fact, they make matters worse. How hard it is to be brave when there is no 'bright side' for us to look on. All of that costs us effort and emotional drain.

Many of us have borne these sufferings for loved ones. Those who have been spared will have to imagine the pain, the inner turmoil, the fear and the anger.

FROM THE BIBLE

MATTHEW 27:38–45

The terrible sequence of events through the Thursday night and Friday morning have now reached their horrific climax. Jesus, having been humiliated and flogged, is crucified. The occupying Roman power does the deed on behalf of those who condemn him, and he is further disgraced by being crucified with two thieves.

For long hours he hangs there nailed to the cross, suffering intensely. Jesus, the Lord of love, now hangs helpless on the cross, his hands and feet pinned by those nails. Jesus, whose loving hands have touched and healed so many—the blind given sight, cripples able to walk, deaf able to hear and the dumb to speak.

Those watching look on silently, helplessly.

'And there was a darkness over the land for three hours.'

MEDITATION

Imagine you are at the terrible scene at Calvary. You see those three figures suffering torment, nailed to crosses.

You wait with the others watching—silently.

What you wanted more than anything else was to bring to Jesus the one you love who is suffering.

It looks like a place of no hope, for Jesus is now utterly unable to help those who need him. His healing, loving hands are pinned with the great nails to the wood of the cross.

Those loving hands had blessed the children, had been held out to Peter as he sank in the waves, had raised the dead daughter of Jairus, had washed the disciples' feet. They had taken and blessed the bread and wine at supper. Now helplessly, painfully, cruelly, those hands are nailed to the cross.

How can Jesus now help you in your agony, as the one you love is suffering?

You address the crucified Lord:

Lord, my world is very black. The one I love is suffering, is in pain. It seems so unfair, so unnecessarily cruel. How can I bear this agony for them?

They do not deserve to suffer; they carry enough burdens in life without this. They don't need this.

Lord, I feel angry, I feel so very angry. How can you let this happen?

You are supposed to be the one who helps those who suffer, the one who heals, the one who makes whole.

Now *you* are helpless—nailed to the cross.

What use are your hands now? You can no longer stretch out your hands to heal, to relieve aching pain and suffering, the torment of loved ones hurting.

Lord, I do not understand. I could bear the pain if it were mine. Why aren't you here, helping and healing those who suffer?

Perhaps, if I could understand that, I might feel a bit better.

I look at you still. What do I see? Is this the end of all your promises? Is there any future for your love, your power to heal? Or is it destroyed for ever?

I look yet again, and I look deeper. What do I see now?

Your suffering is costing you a great deal. So why are you doing it?

Perhaps you are bearing more than your own pain and suffering.

Perhaps you are carrying the hurts and wounds of us all. Is this love poured out in sacrifice?

Maybe you are even carrying the suffering of the one I love—and perhaps my hurts and anger too.

Is it possible that you are bearing the sufferings of the whole world?

And is it possible that you are there with those who are hurting—even the one I love—sharing and bearing their pain? And my hurts and pains too?

Lord, I believe. Please help my unbelief. Help me to trust you, to hold fast to your love which holds me to you.

Help me to know that your hands outstretched on the cross are also outstretched to support us, those wounded hands open still to heal, to make whole.

Lord, I believe. Lord, I trust you. Lord, I hold fast to your love and your power to heal. I feel your pain healing my anger and hurt.

✛

Lord, help us to know that you are here with us as we long to bear the pain of our loved ones for them. Give us faith to know that you are there, bearing their pain and sharing our agonies.

26

SPRING: THE BEAUTY OF THE WORLD

REFLECTION / DISCUSSION

A day comes in the early part of the year when the annual miracle of spring touches God's world and touches us. There is a warmth in the sun, a special kind of blue in the sky, and a fresh vitality in the air.

The trees wear a splendid range of greens and other hues. Blossom and scent are all around—bright yellow daffodils in particular, and countless other beautiful spring flowers. Trees and shrubs suddenly blossom and burst into flower—almost break into song!

And the birds sing—how they sing! If you live in the country, you are blessed indeed with birdsong from very early in the morning, and then late into the evening. Even if you are a town dweller, you hear birdsong in the squares and parks, in the gardens, in the trees alongside some roads. The freshness penetrates the town atmosphere and the air feels cleaner to breathe.

All kinds of happy signs tell us that spring is here. We hear the early cuckoo, the blossom is buzzing with the bees at work, the first swallows and house martins put in an appearance.

There is a new vigour in everyone's step; people sense the joyfulness of the spring season, and the freshness filters into almost everyone's heart. People have a new energy, a spring-cleaning energy. And the drab, bare branches, the empty flowerbeds, the muddy grass—all are transformed by new growth and glorious blossom.

What do you see in the spring? And how do you feel?

FROM THE BIBLE

PSALM 19:1–6; LUKE 24:1–12, 34–36

The first part of Psalm 19 celebrates the glory of God's handiwork. The heavens declare the glory of God and the skies show his handiwork. There is no actual speech, but the glory of God's creation has its own language of beauty, and sings aloud God's praises.

Although there was no thunder and lightning, and no earthquake, the glory of the risen Christ erupted on that first Easter day, a spring day, with great joy. They went to the tomb, those good brave women, to honour the dead body of Jesus. They were overwhelmed as they discovered the great truth—Jesus had risen from the dead.

Later that same day, the disciples were hiding away, but wondering what had happened, because they had heard stories of his resurrection. Even while they were speaking, Jesus came and stood among them. He gave them his greeting: 'Peace be with you.' When at last the truth had sunk in, their joy was unbounded. What a time to celebrate! Out of the misery of death and apparent ending, new life had sprung, and this would be new life for each of them—a total and wonderful transformation.

MEDITATION

Picture yourself on a spring day. Imagine the blossom, the many kinds of flowers, the trees with all the various greens and other colours clothing them.

Perhaps you can sense the freshness of the air, and the perfume of the flowers.

Try to take in the feeling that everything around is very much alive, bursting with fresh growth.

Feel the glorious sense of how all that had seemed dead is now brimming with new life.

Rest for a moment in this exhilarating feeling.

Now think back over your experience of Jesus in your life. Recall how at various times you have been especially aware of his presence and his working in you.

At particular times Jesus has somehow come very much alive in you, bringing you a sense of renewal, of new life, of new joy.

You may have experienced a moment of conversion—a total turning around, a new direction. You may have experienced a gradual growth in your Christian life from your earliest days.

But throughout your life as a Christian, you will have experienced moments of special growth, of transformation.

Think of one of these particular moments in your life when Jesus has seemed very close—a moment of growth, of fresh new life in you. The risen Lord has come to you and filled you with his wonderful peace and joy.

Let one of those moments fill your heart and mind as you think of the new growth of spring. Allow the beauty and freshness of it to flood over you, and let your heart be lifted up to the Lord.

The new world of spring tells out the greatness and glory of the resurrection of Jesus. Every new plant and flower tells of the glorious new life in Jesus Christ that springs out of death.

The risen Lord is very close. We share the surprise and wonder of the women who found the tomb empty that first Easter morning. Our hearts are uplifted as we share their joy.

We share with the gathering of his followers in the evening as they too are gripped by the news.

We are overwhelmed with the wonder of his presence as he comes among us and gives that marvellous greeting, 'Peace be with you.'

Peace enfolds us as we share the spring time of his new life. We rejoice as the spring-time world around us sings of his glory; we rejoice at his vibrant, energizing new life in us, recreating us in his risen likeness.

Jesus Christ is risen. Alleluia, alleluia!

Glorious and holiest God, we praise and thank you for new life in Jesus. We rejoice in his resurrection, symbolized in the beauty of spring time.

27

THE NEWS: VIOLENCE

REFLECTION / DISCUSSION

There is no doubt that we live in a violent age. Not a day goes by without a newspaper report that horrifies us and makes us wonder how people—made in the image of God—can do such dreadful things.

Much of the violence is hidden in statistics—how many have been mugged and robbed, how many have suffered a violent burglary, and how many have suffered all the other crimes. We hear reports of violence between gangs, of racial violence, of houses and even people set on fire. And of course there are many examples of violence among football hooligans.

Other reports hit the headlines. A young boy or girl is murdered, perhaps even by other young boys or girls, or a child is abducted by a paedophile. Our hearts bleed for the distraught parents—we can hardly imagine how devastating it is for them, how the rest of their lives will be shadowed and shattered by what has happened.

Then we hear reports of child abuse—parents or foster parents who are horribly cruel to an innocent child, and children who, if they survive, will be seriously scarred for the rest of their lives. So too with victims of rape: there may be no true recovery—that hideous crime will hurt them and haunt them for the rest of their lives.

All this is just in our part of the world. Elsewhere people suffer appalling torture and unjust imprisonment. We hear of unspeakable horror and cruelty—people's inhumanity to fellow humans. How can we cope with this? How can we live in peace in such a world? And where is God in all of it?

FROM THE BIBLE

MATTHEW 2:16–18; MARK 15:15–34

Soon after Jesus was born, King Herod got to hear about a new 'king'. Brimful of jealousy, he cunningly tried to get the wise men to call back and tell him precisely where the child was. He said that he wanted to come and worship Jesus too, but he was really intent on evil.

The wise men were warned in a dream, and went back home without calling on Herod in Jerusalem. So Herod decided to make quite sure that the child 'king' did not survive, and got his soldiers to kill every male child under the age of two in Bethlehem. It was a devastating act of cruelty for all those families. It became a town in deep mourning throughout their lifetimes.

Jesus survived, but his enemies had a cruel fate in store for him. After he was betrayed, he was tortured—a Roman flogging was quite unspeakable torture. He was made to carry his cross to the killing fields, and then he was put to a hideous death, nailed to a cross and left hanging in agony for some hours before he died. Meanwhile, his enemies mocked him, pouring scorn on his claim to be the Christ. He died in disgrace, a criminal's death, utterly discredited.

MEDITATION

Imagine you are a parent living in Bethlehem. You have a small house, and you have children, including a baby boy of one year old. Life is peaceful. The Roman soldiers seem to stay mainly in Jerusalem, so they don't trouble you.

One winter's day, there are some strange happenings in Bethlehem. It all starts with the census, when so many people flood into the town from far and wide.

Among them is a young woman who can't find anywhere to stay and gets put up in the stable at the inn. There her baby is born, and that's when things begin to happen.

First there is a night of extraordinary bright lights, and some of the shepherds, who should be out in the fields with their sheep, come running into the town with stories that this baby is the promised Messiah. In fact, they wake the whole town in the middle of the night.

Next, some strangers from the East arrive, richly clad, and bringing unusual gifts for the child Jesus. They came through Jerusalem, with directions from King Herod, but they don't go back that way. Apparently Herod was jealous of the baby.

Then the most terrible thing happens. Soldiers of Herod come crashing into the town and, without warning, invade every house and murder every single baby boy.

You will never forget the terror of that night—the shock, and the horror. Your own baby boy is killed, murdered along with all the othes. You are devastated.

You all cry for many days. How could God let such senseless violence happen? You will never get over the pain and grief.

Yet apparently the baby from the stable was not killed. The parents escaped with him.

Many years later, you hear that this Jesus, who now claims to be the Messiah, has been preaching and teaching up and down the country. You see and hear him, and try to follow him as much as you can.

He is a wonderful leader, holy and gifted, healing many sick people. He clearly comes from God. But his enemies capture him, and this time they make no mistake.

After a sort of trial, you follow Jesus as he carries his cross to the place outside Jerusalem where they will put him to death. It is a scene of horror.

The soldiers hammer great nails into his wrists and ankles. This most appalling cruelty is daily work for them. Jesus prays to his heavenly Father for their forgiveness.

Torn and bleeding from the torture, Jesus hangs on the cross for those long hours, which must seem like a lifetime of unremitting pain. Such an act of cruelty and violence.

Only later do you learn that Jesus bears not only the physical pain, but also all the sin and hatred, cruelty and violence that ever was or is. He carries it all, in his love for humankind.

The weight of it all is beyond belief, and he bears it all.

Whenever and wherever violence happens, Jesus is there. He is there in love, bearing the pain and carrying the grief, and praying forgiveness for those who commit violence.

When we think of the unspeakable cruelty and violence of humankind, we are horrified, deeply pained.

We bring to mind the cross of Jesus, and the way he carried all acts of violence, forgiving those who commit such acts. As we pray for those who suffer violence, and for those who commit violence, we think of Jesus bearing that pain and horror on the cross.

We pray for help to see how evil deeds are so often matched by good. The man in the Gospel story who was mugged was given help—quite unexpectedly, courageously and generously—from a stranger and outcast.

We seldom hear or read reports of the good that people do. For a moment, we focus on them too—the many 'good Samaritans'.

Now and again there are television programmes on people who have been generous, or exceptionally kind and thoughtful; and sometimes there are those who have been selflessly courageous—a contrast to the deeds of violence.

We thank God for the millions of acts of kindness, generosity and courage as, day after day, countless people do countless unsung deeds of good.

These are the resurrection people, the ones who help God's goodness to shine through the darkness of violent deeds, and bring light and hope to God's world.

✦

Lord, help us to pray so that the evil of violence can be overcome by good. Lord, help us to see that, in the end, the victory is yours through the cross of Jesus and his resurrection from the dead.

28

RECOVERY

REFLECTION / DISCUSSION

We all suffer at different times and in many different ways. We, or our friend or relation, may be ill—a simple cold, flu, pneumonia, or a variety of diseases and disorders, some very serious. We or others may be hurt in some way—broken bones, sprains, or multiple injuries from a car crash or other accident. Then there is mental illness of various kinds, always distressing because even today, people understand so little, and many still find it hard to have sympathy.

We may be carrying some problem which almost overwhelms us, or we may be weighed down, burdene d for ourselves or for someone else. We may simply be feeling low or sad, feeling that life is not going right for us or for our loved ones, and praying that God will lift up our hearts.

These difficulties may be spread over a long or a short time. But then comes release, recovery. It may be quite unexpected—a healing that is nothing short of miraculous; a solution to a problem that has been paining us for a long time; a burden lifted from us when perhaps we thought there was no solution.

At other times, recovery may be slow and perhaps painful. But it is recovery; and after a time we can look back and say how much better we feel, how relieved we are that circumstances have changed. Recovery is a bright part of many lives, but we do not always remember the source of our recovery. What is your experience of recovery?

FROM THE BIBLE

ACTS 3:1–16

The disciples of Jesus, gifted with the Holy Spirit, continued to preach the good news of Jesus, raised from the dead, and in his name they healed the sick. On one occasion Peter and John were going to the temple at the hour of prayer, through the entrance called the Beautiful Gate.

As they went in, some people came along with a man who had been lame all his life. They would bring him daily to beg for money, so when he saw Peter and John, he asked them for money. But Peter and John looked at him intently, and Peter said, 'I don't have any money to give you, but what I have I give you. In the name of Jesus Christ of Nazareth, stand up and walk.' Peter took him by the hand and lifted him up. Immediately his feet and ankles were made strong and he walked.

He came into the temple with them, leaping and praising God. All the people recognized him and they were awed and amazed.

Peter told the people that it was not their own power that had healed the man, but the name of Jesus—who had been handed over to Pilate and put to death, but whom God raised from the dead.

MEDITATION

Imagine that you are a young man who has been crippled since birth. You cannot walk because there is something very wrong with your feet and ankles; you cannot even stand up. All your life you have been carried wherever you have to go, and you need help from others just to survive.

Your parents have died, so you rely on friends to look after you, but as you cannot work, you have to beg for your living.

That's hard, and never gets any easier. You don't want people to feel sorry for you, but they will only give money if they see your need.

Each day, your friends carry you to a good place at the temple. It's in one of the gateways, sheltered from the sun's heat and from the rain. The gate has a lovely name—it's called the Beautiful Gate.

Day after tedious day, you sit there, calling out to each passer-by. A number of them know you quite well, as they regularly come to the temple to worship. It's good to be greeted by name, even if they have nothing to give you.

Some people, though, can be quite surly. There's the old idea that illness, especially being blind or crippled, is the result of sin, and is a punishment from God. That's hard, and your overall feelings are of hopelessness and despair.

One day, two men come by—Galileans, judging by their accents. You have to try everyone, and chance a surly response.

'Alms, please,' you beg. 'Please spare some money for a poor cripple.'

They stop. No hand pulls out a coin. What will they say?

One of them gives you a searching look—not unkind; in fact, an encouraging and understanding look.

Then he speaks. 'We have no money to give you,' he says, 'but what we do have, we gladly give you. In the name of Jesus Christ of Nazareth, I say to you: stand up and walk!'

You are startled. What can this mean?

Next, however, the man surprises you even more. He reaches out a hand and, taking hold of your hand, he lifts you up. What is happening?

He brings you upright—the first time ever—and then, quite extraordinarily, your ankles and feet have changed. They are now strong; they can support you.

You walk; you take several steps. This is wonderful beyond belief.

You dance around and then follow the two men into the temple, leaping about and praising God.

There are people in the temple who recognize you—your 'regulars', as it were. They are astounded to see you walking and leaping.

You are holding on to the two people—Peter and John, you learn to call them. But Peter, the one who had spoken to you, addresses all the people.

It was not by their own strength or skill that they had healed you, he tells them. It was in the name of Jesus—Jesus who had been killed by the people, but whom God had raised from the dead.

How wonderful is God's love!

Now think of a time in your life when you experienced a recovery. It may be your own or someone else's recovery—from an illness, perhaps, or release from some kind of burden.

Try to recall the feelings of relief at the recovery, of feeling so good that all was now well.

Bring into those feelings the joy of the young man healed by the name of Jesus after a lifetime of being crippled.

Think of the recovery as a celebration, and imagine dancing for joy with the young man in the temple as you too now celebrate release.

Rejoice in the power and love of God, and his resurrection healing grace in Jesus.

✜

Loving Father, we thank you for the power of Jesus to heal, for the resurrection joy of recovery from illness and release from earthly burdens.

29

MEETINGS

REFLECTION / DISCUSSION

There are thousands of meetings every day and in every country throughout the world. Most are business meetings or meetings of people involved in the public services, but every club, society and organization has its meetings—committee meetings, annual meetings, council meetings, open meetings, closed meetings, sub-committees, parent–teacher meetings, action groups, church meetings, briefing meetings.

Normally only one person at a time can speak during a meeting, which means that the rest of the people are silent and supposedly listening. But the boredom factor can be high, and all too often people lose interest, get fidgety, drift into other thoughts, or even fall asleep.

Another aspect of meetings is the politics—the attempts to use the meeting to get our own way, to persuade people who have their own viewpoint, to get or retain power. There are meetings within meetings, or meetings before the main meeting to decide how to manage the politics. So there are fudges, grey areas, perhaps unfair decisions. These kinds of meetings can leave a bad taste in the mouth.

How do we behave in meetings? Are we bossy? Do we talk too much or too little? Do we have an opinion, but fail to express it? Do we fail to listen? Or are we just bored, watching the clock? What, then, is your experience of meetings?

FROM THE BIBLE

LUKE 9:18–21; ACTS 15:6–21

Jesus taught his disciples and trained them. He encouraged them to ask questions—and they did. What was the meaning of this parable or that? they would ask; and he would explain.

Jesus also asked his disciples who people thought he was. They gave various responses, such as 'Elijah', or 'one of the prophets'. But when he asked them who *they* thought he was, Peter—with insight—blurted out that he was the Christ, the Messiah of God.

After his resurrection, Jesus met his followers again in a different way and commissioned them to go out and continue his work. This was confirmed by the coming of the Holy Spirit.

The apostles held meetings, recorded in the book of Acts, which show that they worked together in the Spirit of Jesus. Worship, the breaking of bread, prayer and teaching were at the centre of their activities. But when there was a problem to be solved they had a full discussion, chaired by James, and reached a fair and Christian conclusion. Surely they were guided by the Holy Spirit.

MEDITATION

Imagine you are one of the close followers of Jesus—perhaps one of the Twelve. To your wonder and astonishment, Jesus, after a cruel death, rises to new life. He tells you that you will now be without him, but he promises you the gift of God's Holy Spirit.

You are indeed empowered by the Spirit. You delight in the gatherings of the Christians for worship and prayer, and you share in the apostles' teaching and the fellowship of the breaking of bread.

One day, Paul and Barnabas arrive in Jerusalem after a short time away in Antioch. You hear that there has been a great deal of dissension in that city—all about whether new Gentile Christians should conform to the Hebrew Law.

The atmosphere is very tense when you arrive in the large upper room for a meeting of the believers. Some of the people there are members of the Pharisee sect, and appear to be spoiling for a fight.

As you join in the prayers that begin the meeting, you ask God that peace may prevail and a right and just decision will be reached.

James and the other elders welcome Paul and Barnabas, and you, along with most of those present, feel thrilled by the news of so many Gentiles becoming Christians.

At this point, those who are members of the Pharisee sect stand up and start banging on about the Law of Moses. 'The Gentiles must be circumcised,' they say.

That seems harsh. How do you feel? Perhaps you are saddened that this joyful news should be overcast by such obsessions with ritual?

James keeps everyone calm, and allows a thorough debate. Everyone is allowed to have their say and is fully involved in the meeting, and all listen while others speak. James turns to each person in turn to ensure that they have been heard.

Then, Peter stands up. He tells of his experience of having been sent by God to the Gentiles. He pleads that no extra burden should be placed on those whom God has called to be followers of Jesus. 'After all,' he says, 'God has made no distinction between them and us.'

You find this very heartening. Surely, you feel, it has to be right that we welcome these new Christians as brothers and sisters.

Then silence falls for a time, as Paul and Barnabas stand up. They tell, with great joy, how God has sent them out to the Gentiles—how he has wonderfully blessed all that they have done. They plead that the Gentiles should be given equal treatment, for this is surely the Lord's will—and that they should not be subject to the Hebrew Law. Surely Jesus has given us a new covenant.

You are thrilled with what they say. Their account is alive with the grace and love of God working in them and in the Gentiles to whom they have preached the gospel, and who have been blessed also with the gift of the Holy Spirit.

You admire the way James ensures that there is a consensus; and how he sums up the discussion with a conclusion, which you all fully understand and agree with. It seems most fair and just, and true to the faith.

The apostles will write a letter setting out the conclusions. You sense that Jesus has been present in the meeting, and that you are all working under the guidance of his Holy Spirit.

Now, in your imagination, move to a meeting of your experience —perhaps a difficult meeting, where there are various opposing views. Perhaps people are trying to hijack the meeting and move it in a direction that suits them, or in such a way that they can enhance their own power.

Picture yourself, then, taking part in the meeting. What are your feelings?

Now allow the Spirit of Jesus to show you how to behave. What will he be telling you to say? How is he influencing your feelings?

After the experience of the meeting with James and the others in Jerusalem, how will you now behave—as a Christian, a follower of Jesus gifted with the Holy Spirit?

Maybe part of what you will now do and say will make you unpopular. How will you handle that? And how will the Holy Spirit help you?

Perhaps the discussion will go against what you believe to be right. How will the Holy Spirit help you with that?

✢

Lord Jesus, you are present at every meeting. Help us to know your presence there. Help us to pray for those who lead meetings. May your Holy Spirit be the true guide at each meeting we share.

30

I AM MOVED

REFLECTION / DISCUSSION

The experience of being moved, in the sense of being touched somehow in our inner being by something utterly beyond us, may be rare for many of us, but it is an experience that we are likely to remember and treasure.

Perhaps many people do not recognize the experience for what it is—being touched by something from another world breaking into ours, the Holy Spirit touching our hearts and minds. Created in the image of God, we all have the ability to become aware of his presence through his Holy Spirit.

The circumstances in which we are moved or touched in this sense are many and various. For some it is a still moment in the countryside, in a garden or in a lovely building. But it may be an unexpected moment anywhere and at any time, even in a busy street, driving the car, somewhere in a crowd, or at our place of work. It is never something we achieve ourselves, though, but rather an unlooked-for gift from God.

Some people are moved by great music, by poetry, art or literature, or by drama or film. Being moved in this sense of being touched in our inner selves may also happen in sudden moments of great joy, perhaps in response to an event in our lives or in the lives of our family or friends.

These moments are seldom dramatic; we can easily set them on one side, discounting their significance. We may be unlikely to report them to others, or discuss them. Yet our being touched in this way is to be treasured, held on to, especially when our faith is being tested.

What is your experience? Can you recall such moments in your life?

FROM THE BIBLE

LUKE 9:28–36

Jesus took just three of his disciples to the top of a mountain to pray. While he was at prayer, his face changed and his clothes became dazzling white. The disciples also saw two others, Moses and Elijah, who appeared in glory, and talked to Jesus.

Peter wanted to hold on to the experience by building shelters for the three of them. The disciples seem to have been overwhelmed by the experience. They heard God speaking as a cloud overshadowed them: 'This is my Son, my chosen one; listen to him.' Then they found themselves alone and with much to ponder as they went back down the mountain.

MEDITATION

Imagine you are James or John, two of the three closest disciples of Jesus. You have been with Jesus for about three years now, and have travelled extensively with him, north to Galilee and south to Judea, stopping at many towns and villages and witnessing wonderful events.

You have grown to admire Jesus as a great leader, a powerful healer, and a man of exceptional kindness and compassion. His teaching has opened your eyes to the things of God, and to his love in Jesus.

Now you follow him up the mountain, along with Peter. You would follow Jesus anywhere, without question, for you are totally devoted to him. The day is calm and fine. As you climb higher, you enjoy being able to see further and further.

You wonder what this is about. Jesus has often gone alone to the mountains or to desert places to pray. Indeed, on one occasion you asked him to teach you all to pray.

Now, he says, he is going up this mountain to pray. Perhaps you will somehow be able to share his prayer. Imagine your thoughts as you climb ever higher—how you long to be part of his prayer!

Finally you reach the top. It is lovely to be in that high place. There are views all round, and the beauty of the day seems enhanced by Jesus. You stand quite still and breathe in the wonderful peace.

After a pause, Jesus goes forward and kneels in prayer. You stand where you are, the three of you, absorbing the silence and letting his prayer somehow enfold you too, in a moment of blissful stillness.

Suddenly something quite unexpected happens. Jesus' face and appearance change to a startling brightness, and his clothes become dazzling white. There is a radiance and brilliance about him which is quite out of this world.

You fall on to your knees, totally awestruck. This seems beyond human experience.

You are aware of glory—glory that is very holy, glory that is totally different from anything you have ever known, very simple and at the same time amazing and utterly mysterious. You are bowed down with wonder.

You are further startled and amazed to see, and somehow to recognize, Moses and Elijah also in glory, talking to Jesus. What can this mean? What can be happening to bring those great figures from former times to this present moment?

Then, in a moment of insight, you see the connection and continuity—for these two men have in their turn experienced directly the holiness of God's presence, been awestruck in wonder.

You are again bowed down by the wonderful mystery of this vision.

Peter speaks. He wants to capture this moment and in some way keep the three figures in glory for ever.

But then a brilliant cloud overshadows you all. You are terrified, and hide your head in your hands, wondering what to expect.

Then a voice from the cloud is saying, 'This is my Son, my chosen one; listen to him.' You dare not look up.

You are still overcome with wonder when, after a long moment of mixed terror and bliss, you at last open your eyes. And there is Jesus alone.

You feel that you have been in a different world—a wonderful place, so close to God.

As you go down the mountain in silence, you have much to ponder. You feel you have been touched and deeply moved by God's holiness.

You reflect on the beauty and glory you have seen, and how you have been transformed by the experience—how you have shared this experience with those great prophets of former times. You reflect on this great wonder.

Now bring to mind a time when you felt moved, touched by something outside yourself, touched in your innermost being. Try to remember how you felt at the time.

Perhaps it was a great moment in music, drama or art; or it may have been a moment of stillness in a busy world, or a moment of intense happiness at some great event.

As you recall that moment, remember how you were deeply moved, aware that God was close to you.

Try to bring the experience of Jesus on the mountain into this memory.

Try to feel the continuity and connection with all the experiences of God's glory in Jesus—sharing your own moment of being moved with the bliss of being with Jesus on the mountain, so close to God, and in company with Moses and Elijah.

Allow God's presence to flow over you and around you.

✛

Lord, help us always to be open to your presence and your glory in moments when we are deeply moved. May we be touched and transformed by your holiness.

RESOURCES FOR EXPLORATION AND GROWTH

To stay alive as Christians, we can never stand still—we need to grow. Many gospel images are all about growth: we are the branches of the vine, with the life of Jesus in us; we are the limbs, hands and feet of the body of Christ. We need food to help us to stay alive, to grow, and the source of all life and growth is God in Jesus Christ, through his Holy Spirit. There are resources for growth in Christ within the community of the church—the fellowship, the shared worship, the sacraments, the preaching of the word.

The fundamental source of nurture for the Christian is the Bible, and we need regular, preferably daily, space to read the Bible, usually with the help of notes such as those of the Bible Reading Fellowship (BRF). And we also need help to grow in our inner life of prayer.

TO HELP YOU DEVELOP YOUR INNER LIFE

Among the thousands of books to help you grow in prayer, here are just a few to get you started. First, a book by a wonderful man— Brother Ramon's *Flame of Sacred Love* (BRF, 1999). Based on themes from John Wesley's hymn 'O Thou who camest from above', this is a very personal book written in the last years of Brother Ramon's life. It expounds the creative love of God and how we can draw closer to the heart of that love through the practice of contemplative prayer.

Of the many books on the prayer of silence, you may like to try *Coming to God: In the Stillness* by Jim Borst (Eagle, 1992). A book that emphasizes the use of a 'mantra' (a repeated word or phrase in the silence) is John Main's *Word into Silence* (DLT, 1980).

Henri Nouwen was a very remarkable man and a most gifted writer.

Of his many books on the life of prayer, a good one to start with is *The Way of the Heart* (DLT, 1996). Look out for other books by him too.

More generally, a modern classic on prayer, and a most inspiring book, is *God of Surprises* by Gerald Hughes (DLT, 1985). Another book to help you adventure into prayer is *Taste and See* by Margaret Silf (DLT, 1999). Chapter 3, called 'Sinking into silence', is a useful and very practical help on ways to inner stillness. All these books give useful references to other helpful books; Margaret Silf mentions another modern classic—Anthony de Mello's *Sadhana: A Way to God* (Image, 1984).

FOOD FOR THE JOURNEY

There are collections of meditations and reflective writing which may help to lead you into stillness and silence. In 1973, Hilary Wakeman wrote to a number of church newspapers suggesting that Christian lay people of all denominations might wish to come together from time to time to share in silent contemplation. The response was overwhelming and the Julian Meetings came into being (after St Julian of Norwich, an inspired and inspiring 14th-century contemplative). By 1997, there were 300 Julian Meetings in the UK alone, and out of the regular magazine the first collection of poetry and prose was made—Robert Llewelyn (ed.), *Circles of Silence* (DLT, 1994). The very first piece by Hilary Wakeman, called 'Beginnings...', contains a most useful section explaining the prayer of silence. This first book was followed by another collection—Hilary Wakeman (ed.), *Circles of Stillness* (DLT, 2002).

Another movement has also produced a collection of meditations and prayerful reflections—the Quiet Garden Movement, which is a scheme for opening gardens for days of prayer and meditation. A book grew out of the experience of helping people use quiet gardens—Brigid Boardman and Philip Jebb, *In a Quiet Garden* (Downside Abbey, 2000).

My earlier book is a collection of meditations on events in the

Gospels using your imagination. *Step into the Light: Praying the Gospels Creatively* (John Henstridge, BRF, 2000) was conceived as a way of helping Christians whose prayer is based only on words to grow into deeper ways of prayer. There is also a fine series called 'Companions for the Journey', each volume of which is based on the life and writings of a great Christian. Examples include Gloria Durka, *Praying with Hildegard of Bingen* (Saint Mary's Press, 1991). You will find a number of other titles in this series, such as Julian of Norwich, John of the Cross, Teresa of Avila and Thomas Merton.

There are some excellent collections of daily reflections available. You could try Henri Nouwen, *Bread for the Journey* (DLT, 1996), which has a year's worth of reflections. You may also find sources for daily reflection and prayer on the internet. A particularly good site is www.jesuit.ie. Click on 'Sacred Space', and then 'Prayer for Today'; you will be guided through a prayer path, with a Bible reading for reflection, and plenty of help if you need it. Other Christian sites are in a general reference book: Vernon Blackmore, *God on the Net* (Marshall Pickering, 2001). Most sites have links to other sites, and you may find helpful paths to explore.

To follow up the Julian Meetings, you can access the website www.julianmeetings.org or e-mail JM@fish.co.uk or write to Julian Meetings, The Rectory, Kingstone, Hereford, HR2 9EY. Information on the Quiet Garden Movement can be found at www.quietgarden.co.uk or e-mail quiet.garden@ukonline.co.uk.

Finally, an excellent book of six months of daily readings is Charles Ringma, *Dare to Journey with Henri Nouwen* (Pinon Press, 2000). Each day has a short Bible reading and a reflection on a theme with a quotation from the writings of Henri Nouwen.

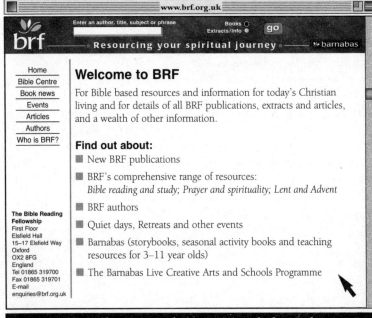